The Nature of Christ

D1279696

*Help for
a church
divided over
perfection*

The Nature of Christ

Roy Adams

REVIEW AND HERALD® PUBLISHING ASSOCIATION
HAGERSTOWN, MD 21740

Copyright © 1994 by
Review and Herald® Publishing Association

The author assumes full responsibility for the accuracy of all facts and quotations as cited in this book.

Scripture quotations marked NASB are from the *New American Standard Bible*, © The Lockman Foundation 1960, 1962, 1963, 1968, 1971, 1972, 1973, 1975, 1977.

Texts credited to NIV are from the *Holy Bible, New International Version*. Copyright © 1973, 1978, 1984, International Bible Society. Used by permission of Zondervan Bible Publishers.

Bible texts credited to RSV are from the Revised Standard Version of the Bible, copyright © 1946, 1952, 1971, by the Division of Christian Education of the National Council of the Churches of Christ in the U.S.A. Used by permission.

This book was
Edited by Richard W. Coffen
Designed by Patricia S. Wegh
Cover design by Bryan Gray
Typeset: 12/13.5 Cochin

PRINTED IN U.S.A.

99 98 97 96 95 94   5 4 3 2 1

R&H Cataloging Service
Adams, Roy, 1941-
     The nature of Christ: help for a
church divided over perfection.

     1. Jesus Christ—Divinity.   2. Perfection—
Religious aspects—Christianity.   I. Title.
          232.8

ISBN 0-8280-0851-5

Dedication

For my wife, Celia,
my children Dwayne and Kim,
and my sisters Mandlyn, Flossie, and Claradell

Contents

Preface

For years now, I have been tracking within the Seventh-day Adventist Church a certain strain of theology centered on Christ's human nature. From North America to the Philippines and from Zimbabwe to Australia, I've watched good Christians go sour as they have delved into the intricacies of this subject. It is a matter to which I do not warm up naturally and, frankly, would rather leave alone. But having sensed the centrality of this issue for a certain segment of our church and the pivotal role it plays in their theology of sin and perfection, I knew that I could not go on ignoring it forever.

The book you now hold in your hand represents a modest effort to bring together my principal reflections on this debate. It is not complete, not by any means, and alert students of theology will immediately notice other chapters or emphases that might have been included. A (positively presented) chapter on justification and sanctification, for example. Or one on eschatology, refuting the unfortunate connection between last-generation perfection and the delay of the Parousia.

What I present here is all that a hectic schedule would permit. I must be content to let others fill in the gaps. To do otherwise—to attempt to be exhaustive against all odds—would risk indefinite setbacks and perhaps even scuttle the work altogether. I believe that the moment to strike is now, and I think that the chapters included here do engage the salient questions of the current debate.

I want to express my profound gratitude to Richard Coffen, William Johnsson, Robert Kloosterhuis, George Knight, and William Shea for taking time from their crushing schedules to read the original manuscript and to share with me their reactions and comments. On a matter as sensitive as the one before us, I found their suggestions and counsel most invaluable. All omissions and blunders, however, are my own.

I'm also grateful to my former secretary, Nicole Bolder Mattox, for her willingness to type and retype the document in the various stages, often deciphering handwritten scribblings only slightly more legible than hieroglyphics.

And a word of deep appreciation to Penny Wheeler, Richard Coffen, Doug Sayles, and others at the Review and Herald Publishing Association who went beyond the call of duty to ensure the timely publication of this work.

Finally and most important—thanks be to God for sustaining grace, enabling power, and spiritual insight.

Special Terms

Brethren	A (usually) lighthearted, playfully pejorative expression used by Adventists to refer to the leaders of the church on various levels and to others. (Even though women are included more and more in leadership positions, no one has yet found a gender-neutral term that carries the playful stab of "brethren.")
Concerned brethren	These members stand in sharp disagreement with church leadership and with the church in general on certain theological and policy issues. Though many of their concerns parallel those championed by the "disaffected brethren," the "concerned brethren" have not openly broken faith with the church and, so far as I know, do not generally espouse or participate in divisive postures or activities. Theological cousins though they may be, the two groups should not, however, be confused.
Disaffected brethren	Refers to those Adventists who, to varying degrees, find themselves in serious disagreement with church leadership or with the church at large on questions of doctrine, strategy, or policy. In open opposition to church leadership, these brethren, in some cases, are developing their own congregations, collecting their own tithes, holding their own camp meetings, publishing their own journals, and even conducting their own ordinations to the gospel ministry.
Spirit of Prophecy	A common expression used by Adventists for the writings of Ellen G. White.
Reform Adventists/ brethren	Some of these would fall in the category of the concerned brethren, others in that of the disaffected brethren. Used here as a catch-all expression.

Introduction

hile studying at Andrews University in the late sixties, I attended an evening presentation given by a visiting Adventist minister in the seminary chapel.* The details of his presentation are gone from me now, but I still recall his major emphases. He referred repeatedly to the historic 1888 Minneapolis General Conference session and claimed that the Adventist Church had rejected the message of righteousness by faith brought to that conference by A. T. Jones and E. J. Waggoner. He spoke of the urgent need for "corporate repentance" on the part of the church for its rejection of the divine message sent to it, and he seemed burdened that the church could never receive the blessing of the latter rain while it remained in its present state of unrepentance and insubordination.

A young seminarian at the time, I vividly remember how puzzled I was as I returned to my room. What on earth was this gentleman talking about? What dark, unknown crime had my church committed of which I was so totally unaware? And what was I to make of his vague hints about some peculiar Adventist brand of righteousness by faith unknown to all other Christians?

If the minister's talk provoked the usual discussions in the seminary halls, I've lost all recollection of them. Nor do I remember hearing in any of my classes specific references to the issues he raised that night. Throughout the years since that presentation, however — through a variety of sources — I have received a good deal of exposure to the things I heard that evening. The mumblings and innuendos have fallen into place, and I now have a fairly good idea of the direction that the speaker was headed. In this book I will attempt to lay out the issues as I see them for the benefit of countless others just as confused now as I was that evening in the late sixties.

Upset by Controversy

Most of us recoil from controversy. We become tired when an issue drags on and on for months. But when it stretches into decades—as in the case of the one before us now—we move beyond fatigue. Our minds shut down, and we feel that we cannot stomach it anymore.

The controversy in our church involving the linkage of *the nature of Christ, sin, sanctification, and perfection* fits this mold. It's been festering for decades now and shows no signs of dying down. For a long time I and many others chose largely to ignore it, hoping that it would go away. But it's not going away. In fact, it's becoming more entrenched in some quarters of the church and confusing more people than ever.

In the fall of 1992, after years of behind-the-scenes "diplomacy," the North American Division of the Seventh-day Adventist Church (NAD) in its year-end meeting finally took action to identify by name certain leading groups among the "reform ministries" that have emerged with a self-appointed mandate to call the Adventist Church to reformation and repentance. The groups singled out were Hope International (based in Eatonville, Washington), Hartland Institute (based in Virginia), and Prophecy Countdown (rooted in central Florida) (see *Issues: The Seventh-day Adventist Church and Certain Private Ministries*, pp. 11-34).

The initial responses to the NAD action were surprisingly positive. The expected backlash did not materialize. But some disagreed, feeling that the groups in question should have been left alone to run their course.

A letter from one of these caught my attention. It referred to Gamaliel's famous statement in the Sanhedrin 2,000 years ago. Gamaliel, after citing examples of failed messiahs, counseled his colleagues on the council concerning the apostles: "Leave these men alone!" he cautioned. "For if their purpose or activity is of human origin, it will fail. But if it is from God, you will not be able to stop" them (Acts 5:38, 39, NIV).

How should we understand the implications of Gamaliel's caution?

Taking Another Look
We need to remember that the fact that Gamaliel's statement appears in the Bible does not necessarily make it true in every partic-

ular. The Bible records—unchallenged—many pronouncements that seem proper but that do not, in their context, necessarily represent the Lord's thinking in every particular. The sentiments of Job's three comforters are a case in point.

So here Luke faithfully reported the words of this wise member of the Sanhedrin, words that successfully restrained the bloodthirsty elements in the council that day. But to reflect on the details of Gamaliel's caution for a little longer than we usually do is to discover that they have not proven true in every historical development.

Consider the second half of the statement first. "But if it [their movement, their cause] is from God, you will not be able to stop" it. This is true in the long term, but not always in the short term. Judeo-Christian history has shown multiplied instances in which God's cause suffered temporary (and sometimes not so temporary) setbacks. The Israelite Egyptian experience, for example. For more than 200 years, some 50 years longer than our own church has existed, God's cause suffered defeat. And for 1,260 years this side of the cross, the necks of God's true people felt the cruel weight of the oppressor's boots—until the liberating light of the Reformation dawned.

Gamaliel's statement was correct—but only in the sense that the church, phoenix-like, rises up again, emerging triumphant from all setbacks. We cannot maintain in the face of history, however, that the enemy never wins a battle against the church. Daniel speaks of a power that will magnify itself "to be equal with the Commander of the host [Jesus Christ]" and that will "fling truth to the ground and perform its will and prosper" (Dan. 8:11, 12, NASB).

What about the *first* part of Gamaliel's statement ("For if their purpose or activity is of human origin, it will fail")? The question is *When* will it fail?

The world around us is filled with wicked, diabolical, godless movements and causes that have persisted now for decades, even centuries. Organized crime is a continuing problem in many countries. Wicked regimes endure while decent ones are overthrown. Many old churches—much older than our own—continue to flourish even if established on unscriptural grounds, some of them wielding great power in the world. Why have they not fizzled out, as

Gamaliel's statement would imply that they should? Is this because they are "from God"? I don't think so.

So we are simply dreaming if we think that the dissident movements among us will simply collapse before our very eyes if we wait long enough. I suspect that they will not—as long as a significant number of our members, unaware of the specious theology on which they thrive, see them as comprising the true Adventist remnant, the loyal upholders of the message of the pioneers, who are gallantly fighting to preserve the church from the clutches of "Calvinism" (whatever that is) and from the "new theology."

That is why I concurred in the action taken by the NAD to make it crystal clear where the church is standing in its relationship to some of these groups. *Issues*, the book produced in connection with that action, is a must-read for every Adventist interested in the phenomenon of contemporary dissident movements among us. It explodes some of the myths propagated by these groups in regard to the positions of "historic Adventism." But whereas *Issues* took the broad-brush approach, I would like to narrow the focus and flesh out in greater detail the theological foundations of these movements. For, in my opinion, unless we do so some of our people will continue to fall prey to this perfectionistic agitation. I think the time has come to deal clearly, unambiguously, and dispassionately with the underlying issues. And that's what I intend to do in these pages. I will make reference to specific individuals whose works are in the public arena, but I will struggle hard to keep such references above the *ad hominem* (or emotionally pejorative) level. These will be objective references—scholarly references, if you please—just as I would treat works by Karl Barth, Albert Schweitzer, Billy Graham, or any other theologian or minister. Disagreement with such published works is not the same as personal dislike for the authors who wrote the citations with which I take issue.

I expect, however, that there will be repercussions. I go into this venture fully knowing the kind of attacks to which I will be subjected. It is a precarious business and one avoided by many Adventist leaders and scholars much wiser and more capable than I.

But I do it for our people. In my travels in recent years, I have listened to questions by the hundreds. And I have always gone away with a keen sense of disappointment because of the partial and disjointed answers that my schedule permitted. Here I would like to spell out more deliberately my position on the many ramifications of the issues that have concerned these earnest fellow believers.

I'm not writing primarily for the benefit of those who have already made up their minds that the church has apostatized or embraced a "new theology." Rather, I'm trying to reach the large majority of our people who have not been infected by the virus of judgmentalism and suspicion. For once one becomes infected, this disease, in my observation, is well-nigh incurable.

I've listened with deep understanding and empathy to those who want to avoid this discussion. To them it looks petty, picayune—even disgusting. And I cannot tell you how often I myself have felt that way. My deep-seated inclination is to leave the matter alone—let it go away, run its own course. But once you take a moment to understand where these movements are coming from, as we say, then you know that they are not about to go away anytime soon. After all, how can you fold up tent and go away when you see yourself as a special remnant, raised up to usher in our Lord's second advent? Why, to fold tent under these circumstances would be treason of the highest order! No, people with such convictions do not simply fade out of the picture. And to expect them to is simply wishful thinking.

Conciliation (part of the "quiet diplomacy" I referred to above) has not worked. Every call by church leaders for unity has met with resistance.

Back in 1990 *Adventist Review* editor William Johnsson called on the church in North America to "press together." On the question of Christ's human nature, he pleaded for all of us to stand together behind our statement of fundamental beliefs—that "Jesus, God's eternal Son, became fully human, was tempted in all points, but remained sinless." And since our beliefs "do not attempt to spell out [Christ's] nature beyond this," it's time to put aside our own cherished view and press together for the rescue of a world "going down to ruin" (*Adventist Review*, Nov. 1, 1990, p. 4).

How was Johnsson's plea received? If the reaction of Donald

K. Short is any indication, not well. Mistakenly attributing the call to the Biblical Research Institute, Short responded as follows: "What truth is essential for salvation? Can anything be more important than knowing the One who is 'the way, the truth, and the life' (John 14:6)? The Scriptures never hint that the nature of Christ is unimportant and therefore can be passed over lightly" (Donald K. Short, *Made Like His Brethren*, p. ix).

To read Short's response carefully is to notice a number of insinuations completely absent from Johnsson's editorial. For example, nothing in the original editorial suggested that there is something more important than knowing Jesus—nor even that "the nature of Christ is unimportant." In a similar way, virtually every other effort at conciliation has been met with resistance and misrepresentation. Surely whatever side we take in these issues, we should be scrupulously concerned with considerations of accuracy and fairness. And it does not appear that confrontation will defeat some people. The martyr complex lies altogether too near the surface—you know, the tendency to envision oneself as suffering for the faith once delivered to the saints.

Knowing all this, I do not have the audacity to think that this little work of mine will make much of a difference within the ranks of some Adventist critics. These seasoned controversialists do not generally concede anything. Whatever the arguments you present, however clear or convincing you make the case and however well supported by Scripture or by Ellen G. White's writings your reasoning, you can be sure that there will be others who will bring forward counterarguments. That's a given.

But I have faith in the power of truth. And I have faith in the rank and file of our people—in their levelheadedness, their savvy, their reasonableness, their good judgment. And I believe that if Seventh-day Adventist leadership candidly presents the issue before them, they'll make the right decisions.

Let me state clearly here at the outset that the perfectionist movement among us does not impress me. Not, I think, because I am stubborn or hardheaded, but because I have taken the time to familiarize myself with the issues concerned and have come to know something of the speciousness and peril of that strain of theology. I want to share what I have found with everyone who cares to know.

---

* I cannot positively identify the speaker after these many years, but I recall that he had served as a missionary in Africa and was on either temporary or permanent return. He might have been Robert Wieland (whom I will be quoting later), but I cannot be absolutely sure.

Chapter 1

HOW THEY SEE IT:
The Theological Reasoning
of the Concerned and Disaffected Brethren

Before taking a few days off work to collect my thoughts for this book, I was clearing away the flood of papers and magazines that had accumulated in my office, when out of one pile dropped a tiny booklet with a title printed in an eye-catching colored ink: *Christ's Human Nature*. The document bore the name of Joe Crews, director of Amazing Facts, an Adventist radio-television evangelistic ministry.

I couldn't remember seeing the booklet before and had no idea how it came to be among my papers. Without the foggiest notion of what it might contain—I'd never heard Crews on that topic before—I took the pamphlet home. And this is how, quite unexpectedly, I came to use it here as a point of departure in reviewing the thinking of a certain segment of our church about Christ's human nature. Just 27 small pages long, Crews's booklet provided a convenient summary of the kind of thinking I wanted to address.

(Obviously, then, I'm *not* hereby including Crews among either the "concerned" or "disaffected" brethren. *I want this to be crystal clear.* So far as I know, when it comes to his relationship with the denomination, Crews is a team player who cooperates in every way that he can. My reference to him here is meant to be objective and scholarly, dealing with his published position on the topic under study. As I pointed out in the introduction, I'm citing his booklet here in the same way that I would quote any other author with whom I may agree or disagree. Amazing Facts was *not* one of the organizations singled out by name by the North American Division in its book *Issues*.)

After alerting his readers that he'd be tackling a most "deadly" religious counterfeit, Crews begins his pamphlet with an attack on the doctrine of original sin. Interjected into early Christianity, he says, this false doctrine teaches "that Adam's guilt was . . . imputed to his descendants." Not so, says Crews. "The valid biblical position," lying close to the counterfeit, holds that man has inherited a "carnal nature, which predisposes him to sin" (Joe Crews, *Christ's Human Nature*, pp. 1, 3). Though "marginal," says Crews, the distinction nevertheless is all-important.

We would have to assume that Crews, while perhaps concerned as an evangelist about Christians in general, really aims his arguments on this point at his fellow Adventists. He wants to correct what he sees as a widespread acceptance among us of the concept of original sin, à la Augustine.

Joe Crews is not alone in his view that the Augustinian emphasis on original sin, in all its ramifications, pervades Adventism. I have run into the charge again and again in the publications of the so-called right-wing groups. For example, in their book *Adventism Vindicated*, Colin and Russell Standish, following a format almost identical to that of Crews on this point, zero in on the concept of original sin at the very beginning of their chapter on Christ's nature: "Many [Adventists?], following part of the Augustinian package of falsehood, teach that Christ's human nature was unfallen. . . . Yet Augustine's position was established upon the false premise of man's original sin" (p. 61).

And Ralph Larson, in *The Word Was Made Flesh*, offers this loaded question as the title to Appendix C: "Should Augustine's Doctrine of Original Sin Be Added to Seventh-day Adventist Theology?" Then he adds: "Since it is common knowledge that Augustine's doctrine of original sin is now being recommended for addition to the theology of the Seventh-day Adventist Church, it would appear that a careful examination of that doctrine should be undertaken by all who share a concern for the purity of the Adventist faith" (p. 330). Larson then proceeds with about 20 pages of discussion on the subject (pp. 330-350). However, his startling allegation here not only is *not* "common knowledge" but is also patently unfounded.

Crews (to return to his outline), after disposing with the doctrine of original sin, turns to the main item on his agenda—Christ's human nature.

The churches of Protestantism, he says, having accepted the unscriptural doctrine of original sin, found themselves forced into an erroneous position about the human nature of Christ—namely, that Christ's sinlessness resulted from His being "born with the unfallen nature of Adam" (*Christ's Human Nature*, pp. 6, 7). Such a doctrine, according to Crews, is "diametrically opposed" to Scripture, which teaches "that Jesus had a human nature *exactly like ours*" (*ibid.*, pp. 7, 8; italics supplied). (In support, Crews quotes such passages as Hebrews 2:11, 16, 17.)

"Exactly like ours." For Crews nothing less and nothing else will do. Turning to Ellen G. White, he quotes the following statement: "It would have been an almost infinite humiliation for the Son of God to take man's nature, even when Adam stood in his innocence in Eden. But Jesus accepted humanity when the race had been weakened by 4,000 years of sin. Like every child of Adam He accepted the results of the working of the great law of heredity. What these results were is shown in the history of His earthly ancestors. He came with such a heredity to share our sorrows and temptations, and to give us the example of a sinless life" (*The Desire of Ages*, p. 49; quoted in *Christ's Human Nature*, p. 12).

Crews's position parallels that of many of our concerned as well as disaffected brethren. Christ assumed "the fallen, sinful nature of man after the Fall," argue Robert J. Wieland and Donald K. Short. "The 1888 message accepts 'likeness' to mean what it says, not *unlikeness*." The teaching "that Christ took only the sinless nature of Adam before the Fall . . . [is] a legacy of Romanism, the insignia of the mystery of iniquity" (*1888 Re-examined: The Story of a Century of Confrontation Between God and His People*, p. iii).

This emphasis is also found in *The Word Was Made Flesh*, a book that claims on its title page to bring together "100 years of Seventh-day Adventist Christology." For hundreds of pages the author, Ralph Larson, hammers home the point that Christ came in fallen human nature—a nature *absolutely* identical to ours. Larson counters again and again the position that the nature Christ took in the Incarnation was that of the unfallen Adam.

The Adventist who has not suspected where these brethren are going with their argumentation will certainly find their approach repetitive—even exasperating. However, once you understand where they're headed, you begin to see that the approach has an internal logic of its own. It becomes clear that by their emphasis on Christ's sameness to us, they want to establish the fundamental point that *what He did, we can do also.*

What confuses some Adventists as they read such literature is that *much of what is said is true and is held by most of us.* But beneath the surface of what might appear to the ordinary reader to be regular Adventist teaching, there is usually a subtle spin. On Christ's temptation, for example, Robert J. Wieland wrote as follows: "Was Christ indeed 'in all points tempted like as we are,' from within as well as from without? Or was He so different from us that He could not feel our inward temptations?" "Could He feel as we feel?" he continued. "Was He really and truly man? Was He tempted only as the sinless Adam was tempted, or was He tempted as *we* are tempted?" (*The 1888 Message: An Introduction,* p. 42).

The ordinary reader would hardly suspect that what Wieland is driving at here is that Christ had a carnal nature, with the same passions as we have—the same propensities, the same bent to evil—and that if He didn't, then He could not have been tempted in all points as we are.

So Wieland's questions are not as innocent and elementary as they may seem at first sight. For him and others who agree with his position, such queries focus attention on the heart of the issue—namely, that Christ came "to rescue man *where he is,* taking upon His sinless nature our sinful nature and experiencing all our temptations within His soul and yet completely triumphing over" them. This, we are told, was the "central heart" of the 1888 message (*ibid.*).

In taking our sinful nature and developing therein "a perfectly sinless character," Christ set an example for us to follow. According to Wieland and Short, "It is impossible to have true New Testament faith in Christ and continue in sin. We cannot excuse continued sinning by saying that we are 'only human'" (*1888 Re-examined*, p. iii). They argue that the high priestly ministry of Christ eventually "must change. . . . He cannot forever minister His blood in substitution to cover the perpetual sinning of His people." He must finish the work of perfection in us, bringing us to a state "never accomplished previously" in any other generation. "He must have a people who overcome 'even as' He overcame, a people who 'condemn sin in the flesh'" (*ibid.*, p. 156).

In what is perhaps the most startling statement any of these brethren has ever made, Wieland and Short declare that "the Second Coming is impossible unless Christ ceases to be our substitute" (*ibid.*, p. 195). I interpret this to mean that we must come to the place where our own condemnation of sin in the flesh is so complete that we have no further need for a high priestly substitute in the heavenly sanctuary. This is truly an amazing statement, and it shows the extremes of which this kind of theology is capable. *Again and again I have noticed what seems to be a diminishing need for Christ in this strain of theology.* Nevertheless, this position, resting as it does on a particular understanding of Christ's human nature, is of absolute importance to this group of Adventist thinkers. That is why Joe Crews, in the pamphlet under discussion, wanted to leave no stone unturned in his emphasis on the absolute identity of Christ's human nature with ours. At one point, arguing the case as though the author of Hebrews wrote in English, he penned the following in commentary on Hebrews 2:14—and the emphases are his: "Notice how the inspired writer emphasized the sameness of the body of Christ with man, HE—ALSO—HIMSELF—LIKEWISE. These four words are used consecutively even though they are repetitive and redundant. WHY? In order to impress us that Jesus really did enter into the SAME nature man possessed" (*Christ's Human Nature*, p. 10). Of course, the apostle did not write in English, and Crews would have done us a service by not giving undue emphasis to what is, in fact, merely a matter of English idiomatic style—now nearly 500 years old. Notice, by way of contrast, the New International Version's rendition of the same text (with the corresponding phrases italicized): "Since the children have flesh and blood, *he too*

Western, corrupted Hort

shared in their humanity so that by his death he might destroy him who holds the power of death—that is, the devil" (Heb. 2:14). The text is surprisingly straightforward. It was meant to express Christ's solidarity with us and the reason for it—namely, that by His death He might destroy the devil.

The kind of emphasis that Crews tries to underline is overblown. It reminds me of the story about a visitor entering a London subway very late at night and encountering a sign that read: "Dogs must be carried on the trains." "For the life of me," he said, "where would I find a dog this hour of the night?" Those who wrote the sign (as well as countless others who'd read it) thought it was clear enough. But someone came along and read something quite foreign into it. Many of our concerned brethren and perhaps most of our disaffected brethren tend to seize selected statements and blow them out of proportion in order to make their case.

non sequitur

Is your only evidence or for the NIV?!

And what is the case they're trying to make? We might summarize it here under four main points:

1. Christ's human nature was exactly like our own—*100 percent*.

2. Since Christ lived a sinless life in fallen human nature—a nature absolutely identical to ours—then we too, depending on the same source of power as He did, can and must live "without sinning." (This, the reformist groups believe, was the theological breakthrough on righteousness by faith that came to Adventists in 1888 and that the corporate Adventist Church has continued to reject.)

3. When the remnant church finally accepts this message and arrives at the stage of absolute sinless perfection, Christ's character will have been fully reproduced in His people, and He will come to claim them as His own.

yes! EGW.

4. As long as the church fails to reach this state of absolute sinless perfection, the latter rain will not fall, the loud cry of Revelation 18 will not be given in its fullness, and Christ will not come.

yes, evidence

Loaded down, as they often are, with a multitude of quotations from Ellen G. White's writings, the arguments appear convincing to some. But have these authors faithfully reckoned with all the facts? Or have they ignored certain crucial evidence that, when taken into account, could severely damage—if not completely destroy—their line of reasoning? *oh good! Show me!!*

The following chapters will address this concern in more detail. But for now, some preliminary observations on this matter of original sin and Christ's human nature.

Preliminary Observations

It's beyond the scope of this study, let alone this chapter, to give a detailed, line-by-line critique of the position of the reform groups. Nor do I feel inclined to point out the shortcomings of their argu- *how about at any turn?!* ments at every turn. But I think it might be helpful to provide just a sampling of the kind of assessment to which some of the foregoing claims and statements might be subjected.

For most of us, the classical doctrine of original sin is rather remote, hardly ever coming to mind in our everyday experience and reflection. For our reform brethren, however, the doctrine constitutes a theological flash point in any discussion about Christ's human nature. For in order to make the point that Christ, in terms of His humanity, was 100 percent like us—*absolutely nothing excepted*—they must first establish the position that we inherit nothing from Adam that intrinsically needs redemption.

I have no inclination to defend the classical doctrine of original sin. Augustine suggested, for example, that original sin is transmitted biologically—through sexual procreation—and that we are born guilty (see Alan Richardson, ed., *A Dictionary of Christian Theology*, p. 204). We should note, however—notwithstanding the continued *sequuera* misrepresentation of certain Adventist authors—that this is not the position of Adventist theologians today nor of theologians on a whole. As William Hordern notes: "Few theologians today accept the view that guilt can be inherited."[1] "But theologians are widely agreed," continues Hordern, "that the state in which we find man is out of harmony with God's will and purpose for him." *And the crucial point is that this is true of the whole human race since the Fall*, with just *one* exception, as we will see.

So I'm not defending here the Augustinian concept of original sin. (What contemporary Adventist Bible student would want to *some apparently do!*

pick up the theological baggage of Augustine or of any other ancient theologian?) But I could not help noticing the vacuousness of the kind of arguments usually marshaled against this teaching that, whether it is correct or in error, was nevertheless articulated by some of the keenest theological minds of the Christian church.

Crews, for example, allows that "Adam's weakened, sinful nature was passed on to his children through the law of heredity, *making it impossible for them not to sin*" (*Christ's Human Nature*, p. 4). Yet he turns around and makes the point that Christ took that very nature, but without falling into sin. How? "Because He was filled with the Holy Spirit from the womb and possessed a fully surrendered will and sanctified human nature" (*ibid.*, p. 15).

"without Christ's power"?

How can one argue, on the one hand, that Christ had to be exactly like us—100 percent—or He could not be our example, and then turn around and suggest that the reason He did not sin is that "He was filled with the Holy Spirit *from the womb*"? The elementary question that must follow from this is Why, then, didn't God give to each of us the same measure of the Holy Spirit—"from the womb"—as He gave to Christ? And wouldn't it have been nice for each of us to start out with a "fully surrendered will," as Crews claimed Christ did?

look this up in Crews book

Here's another example. As Wieland and Short tried to develop their emphasis on our responsibility for what happened in 1888 and our need for corporate repentance, their position on original sin seemed to backfire on them. Notice the curious argument by which they tried to get around the problem.

"We today inherit no genetic guilt of our forefathers [of 1888] who rejected the grandest opportunity of the ages, the beginning of the latter rain and the loud cry; but we are their spiritual descendants. Holy Scripture teaches no genetic transmission of sin, 'original' or otherwise, from generation to generation. *But there is a transmission of sin which is not genetic.* 'By one man sin entered into the world.' 'Sin abounded' and 'hath reigned unto death.' 'All the world [has] become guilty before God' (Romans 5:12, 20, 21; 3:19)" (*1888 Re-examined*, p. 77; italics supplied).

sounds like the grafted-limb don't apply to me

What curious reasoning! And one would think that the person expounding it would look for some kind of backing, however weak,

[handwritten marginalia: "Wieland & Short don't speak for me"]

for such pronouncements. But no, Wieland and Short simply sug-
gest that it is a "mysterious transmission" (*ibid.*).[2] *[handwritten: "no it doesn't!"]*

The kind of reasoning displayed in these examples permeates
the writings of many concerned Adventists as well as dissident
brethren. They argue against the so-called prelapsarian position in
regard to Christ's human nature—the view that Christ took the nature of Adam before the Fall (before Adam *lapsed* into sin, in other
words). Short sees a "growing dichotomy in the [Adventist] church
today." "There is outright objection," he says, "to Christ taking
fallen human nature. Many insist on holding the pagan philosophy
of Babylon that proclaims God's dwelling is not with 'flesh' (Daniel
2:11). (The only kind of 'flesh' there is in the world is fallen human
flesh.)" (*Made Like His Brethren*, p. 139).

The confusion here is immense. But I simply call attention to the
first part of the statement and ask Who are these people really fight-
ing? Unless I have it all wrong, I don't run into many Adventists de- *[handwritten: "aren't"]*
fending a prelapsarian position. And in all the samplings I've done
in preparation for this book, I've not seen a single instance in which *[handwritten: "NOT TRUE!"]*
one of our concerned or disaffected brethren has managed to pro-
duce a direct prelapsarian statement from a contemporary
Adventist author. *[handwritten: "OK, evidence to go here: Gillian & Desmond"]*

But apparently, notwithstanding the absence of direct evidence,
these authors are discovering such materials all the time. Why else
would Ralph Larson devote more than 133 pages to emphasize that
Adventists for 100 years had been teaching (to use just one of the
hundreds of quotations he marshals) that Christ took "upon
Himself the form and nature of fallen man"? (*The Word Was Made
Flesh*, p. 35; cf. pp. 34-66, 111, 212).

As I read the publications produced by these and other re-
formists, I have been astonished at the time and effort that obviously
went into making a point that I would have thought was elementary *[handwritten: "I'm glad!"]*
for most, if not all, Adventists. *We believe—and have always believed—* *[handwritten: "Now let's document how wrong you are!"]*
that Christ did take upon Himself the form and nature of fallen human beings!
Why expend so much time and effort preaching to the choir?

Through all this effort, Larson and his colleagues are laboring
with the false assumption that everyone who fails to accept their po- *[handwritten: "says who?"]*

sition—in its entirety—thereby automatically falls into the prelapsarian camp. I cannot imagine that all these brethren, focusing for all these years on this subject as intensely as they have, could have failed to notice that there is a *third option.* I also find their silence on this third option astonishing. *AH!*

But there is, of course, a third option, and we are inching our way toward it.

---

[1] Bear in mind, however, that the word "guilt may be used in different contexts with important differences in meaning" *(A Dictionary of Christian Theology,* p. 149). And we find Ellen G. White herself employing the word, as we shall see in chapter 4, to describe something that we inherit from our forebears.

[2] Some of the same inconsistencies may be found in Wieland, *Corporate Repentance,* pp. 77, 79, 118.

Chapter 2

EXAMINING THE ROOTS:
The Legacy of Jones
and Waggoner

I n any attempt to understand an issue, one must try to trace its underlying roots. This chapter will look back at A. T. Jones and E. J. Waggoner. Chapter 3 will take up the legacy of M. L. Andreasen. My thesis throughout is that the theology of these three men has provided the spawning ground for the position on righteousness by faith and perfection held by certain Adventists today.

In preparing this chapter, I have relied heavily on George Knight's well-documented historical-theological assessment of A. T. Jones.[1] Knight has done the Adventist Church an invaluable service in this work.

A Fascination for 1888

One cannot read the publications of many on the Adventist right for very long without detecting a fascination with the Minneapolis General Conference session of 1888. Everything seems to center on what happened there. These authors focus particularly on the two young preachers who featured most prominently in the theological debates which rocked that historic session.

Without a doubt, the roots of the present agitation go all the way back to Jones and Waggoner. Donald K. Short's high valuation of Jones and Waggoner, to use one example, makes their pivotal role abundantly clear. He begins by comparing the eventual fall of Jones and Waggoner to the great disappointment of 1844. "Both [events] are embarrassing," he says, "and both require understanding . . . [lest we] make serious mistakes." Reflecting on these two events (1844 and 1888), Short makes the following statement: "It seems that the Lord Himself has permitted both as an almost over-mastering point of confusion and a stumbling block to anyone who is looking for an excuse to reject truth" (*The 1888 Message*, p. 66).

According to Short, Jones and Waggoner had been "forced to endure 'unchristlike persecution' from their brethren," "pressures that no others have been called to endure in quite the same way" (*ibid.*, p. 67). "In comparison with Jones and Waggoner," said Short, "Luther had a relatively easy problem in meeting the virulent opposition of the Papacy and Catholic hierarchy toward his message" (*ibid.*, p. 68).[2]

So why did Jones and Waggoner apostatize? Not because of any "extreme views" on their part regarding righteousness by faith, reasoned Wieland and Short. Rather, "they were *driven away* by the persistent and unreasoning opposition of the brethren whom God sent them to enlighten" (*1888 Re-examined*, p. 116). As He did for Moses who had been brought down by an ungrateful people, God "buried" His messengers (Jones and Waggoner) "secretly," removing thereby "all occasion for idolatry" from coming generations (*ibid.*, p. 123).

That last remark is followed by this puzzling statement: "What better method of 'burial' than to allow the messengers to lose their way in disgrace?" (*ibid.*). I interpret this to mean that out of concern for us God allowed Jones and Waggoner to fall in order that we might not idolize them! What a terrible characterization of God!

This larger-than-life approach to Jones and Waggoner is designed to heighten the significance of their 1888 message. So important is this message that "before the time of final victory," it will be necessary that the remnant church come to understand the truth that it contains "and recognize Jones' and Waggoner's work . . . for its true value, the 'beginning' of the latter rain and the loud cry" (*ibid.*, p. 117).

Identifying the Message

What, then, were the messages that Jones and Waggoner brought to the 1888 session? The first thing to note is that *we have no record* of what they said. The undisputed fact is that their presentations were not written down. Short acknowledges this when he says that "we really do not have the 1888 message itself in the exact words of the two young messengers at Minneapolis" (*The 1888 Message*, p. 9).[3]

Though we do not have these messages, it is clearly in the interest of the right wing to reconstruct them as nearly as they can, so as to capitalize on Ellen White's ringing endorsement of them. Otherwise they are faced with the unenviable problem of having the prophet's strong endorsement, but not the thing the prophet endorsed.

In their attempt to reconstruct these messages, however, they have managed to read back into 1888 some of the later emphases of Jones and Waggoner. This has resulted, among other things, in a *strong stress on Christ's human nature*, since that was one of the prominent themes developed by the two brethren in the post-1888 period.

According to Knight, by 1895 Jones had come to see *"the total likeness of Christ's nature to that of other humans as central to his presentation of righteousness by faith"* (*From 1888 to Apostasy*, p. 136). Said Jones in his address to the *1895* General Conference delegates: "Christ's nature is precisely our nature. In His human nature there is not a particle of difference between him and you" (1895 *General Conference Bulletin*, pp. 231, 233, 436; cf. *From 1888 to Apostasy*, p. 136).

And what did Jones make of this absolute likeness? "In Jesus Christ as He was in sinful flesh, God has demonstrated before the universe that He can so take possession of sinful flesh as to manifest His own presence, His power, and His glory, instead of sin manifesting itself. And all that the Son asks of any man, in order to accomplish this in him, is that the man will let the Lord have him as the Lord Jesus did" (*ibid.*, p. 138).

By thus overcoming sin in sinful flesh, Jones concluded, Jesus has opened a "consecrated way" for each of us to do the same (see *From 1888 to Apostasy*, p. 138). So, then, when our concerned and disaffected brethren refer to "the 1888 message," this is the emphasis they generally have in mind. Like Jones, they would point out that if Christ gained the victory in human flesh, with a nature exactly (100 percent) like ours, then we can have no excuse for not gaining a similar victory and thereby live without sin.

If we think we can coax them to abandon this emphasis "for the sake of peace and unity," then we really do not understand the depth of their conviction. For them, Christ's fallen human nature is the fundamental, undergirding rationale for the whole framework of their theology. It is a dimension, moreover, that assumes cosmic proportions because it ties in with the cleansing of the sanctuary, the perfecting of a final remnant, and Jesus' second coming.

Some Problems With This View

This approach, however, faces several complications.

1. As already indicated, the actual messages of both Jones and Waggoner at the 1888 session were never recorded. (Some Adventists today see this as providential—"one of the best things that happened to the 1888 message," says Knight [*From 1888 to Apostasy*, p. 70].) This means that there is no way of discovering what Jones and Waggoner actually said and that, therefore, we cannot be sure about what precisely was included in Ellen White's endorsement.

2. Even if we had actual copies of Jones's and Waggoner's presentations and even if those presentations included references to the human nature of Christ, we still could not be sure that their emphasis on Christ's human nature was, necessarily, included in Ellen White's approval. For example, when early in her ministry she endorsed O.R.L. Crosier's landmark article on the sanctuary, she obviously did not mean to endorse also his erroneous views on "the age to come" appearing in the same article.[4]

3. Moreover, we have explicit evidence that Ellen White's endorsement of Jones's and Waggoner's messages was not completely without equivocation. "She freely told the assembled delegates on November 1, 1888, that 'some interpretations of Scripture, given by Dr. Waggoner, I do not regard as correct'" (*From 1888 to Apostasy*, p. 72; cf. E. G. White manuscript 15, 1888).

A little more than a year later, she expressed similar sentiments to a group of ministers about both Jones and Waggoner: "I believe without doubt that God has given precious truth at the right time to Brother Jones and Brother Waggoner. Do I place them as infallible? Do I say that they will not make a statement, nor have an idea that cannot be questioned? or that can not be error? Do I say so? — No, I do not say any such thing. . . . But I do say God has sent light" (manuscript 56, 1890, quoted in *From 1888 to Apostasy*, p. 72).

Since Ellen White gave only general endorsement of the messages of Jones and Waggoner, without specifying her position on the details, we could not assume that we know her position on anything beyond the *central point* of their messages, even if we had the written documents.

In other words, we must not look upon Ellen G. White's endorsement of these two men "as a kind of blank check in doctrinal matters," writes Knight, noting in this connection two areas of Waggoner's Christology that she could not have endorsed. Waggoner, in 1889, had taken the position that it was impossible for Christ to sin (*Signs of the Times*, Jan. 21, 1889, p. 39) and (in an 1890 book) that He did have a beginning (E. J. Waggoner, *Christ and His Righteousness*, pp. 20-22; cf. Knight, *Angry Saints*, pp. 44, 45).

Knight is correct, of course. In *The Desire of Ages* (published in 1898), she loudly proclaimed that "in Christ is life, original, unborrowed, underived" (p. 530). And, as we will note in chapter 5, she clearly indicated that it was possible for Jesus to sin.

4. The human nature of Christ was most probably *not discussed* at the 1888 Conference. After examining two new sources of information on the famous council (the diary of R. Dewitt Hottel, giving a day-by-day report of the topics covered, and two booklets of notes by W. C. White taken during the meetings) as well as extensive correspondence bearing on the 1888 General Conference agenda, Knight reached the following conclusion: "None of these records demonstrate that the divinity of Christ, the human nature of Christ, or 'sinless living' were topics of emphasis or discussion at the 1888 meetings" (*From 1888 to Apostasy*, p. 37). Bending over backward, as it were, Knight, in a personal letter to me, conceded to "have now uncovered some evidence that . . . [these subjects] had at least come up." But he maintains that they were certainly "not matters of emphasis."

This conclusion appears to find confirmation in an Ellen G. White 1891 diary entry. In that entry, which Knight regards as a possible "distillation of the heart of the 1888 message," she focused on the blending of law and gospel—an emphasis that had been lost in Adventism because of the church's past preoccupation with the law only.

The overriding burden in the diary entry was on love and kindness and practical godliness. "The religion of many is very much like an icicle," she wrote, "freezingly cold. . . . They cannot touch the hearts of others, because their own hearts are not surcharged with the blessed love that flows from the heart of Christ. There are others," White continued, "who speak of religion as a matter of the will. They dwell upon stern duty as if it were a master ruling with a scepter of iron—a master stern, inflexible, all-powerful, devoid of the sweet, melting love and tender compassion of Christ" (E. G. White diary, Feb. 27, 1891, cited in Knight, *From 1888 to Apostasy*, pp. 68, 69).

So in other words, Ellen White's overriding concern during the 1888 period was with practical Christianity, practical godliness. Not that she was uninterested in doctrine, as such. But her concern for doctrine was related to the manifestation of that doctrine in the life and work of God's people. I think it is impossible to demonstrate from her diary (and other) summaries of the 1888 experience any concern for topics such as sinlessness or the nature of Christ.

They Remain Unmoved

It is discouraging business to write on these topics. George Knight's book, with all its documentation, apparently has not moved some readers one iota. The spirit of accusation and suspicion continues on apace. The fact that *we do not have* the messages that Ellen G. White endorsed does not detain such enthusiasm. To my knowledge, not one significant right-wing proponent has conceded a single theological point, notwithstanding the presentation of the most compelling historical and theological evidence.

Perhaps that should not surprise us. It's very humbling to admit error on a point one has invested years of time and effort defending. After he had emphasized Christ's absolute oneness with us in one of his sermons at the 1895 General Conference session, Jones was confronted by some delegates with an Ellen G. White statement to the effect that Christ "is a brother in our infirmities, but not in possessing like passions" (see *Testimonies*, vol. 2, p. 202).

Jones's response was the typical one we find today. He tried to circumvent the issue. His approach was to differentiate "between Christ's flesh and His mind" (*From 1888 to Apostasy*, p. 138).

In the meeting following the one at which the question had been raised, Jones offered this surprising explanation: "Now as to Christ's not having 'like passions' with us: In the Scriptures all the way through He is like us, and with us according to the flesh. . . . *Don't go too far.* He was made in the likeness of sinful flesh; *not in the likeness of sinful mind. Do not drag His mind into it.* His flesh was our flesh; but the mind was 'the mind of Christ Jesus.' . . . If He had taken our mind, how, then, could we ever have been exhorted to 'let this mind be in you, which was also in Christ Jesus'? It would have been so already. But what kind of mind is ours? O, it is corrupted with sin also" (*General Conference Bulletin*, 1895, pp. 312, 327; italics supplied; see *From 1888 to Apostasy*, p. 138).

But isn't my mind part of my sinful, fallen nature? And isn't it the mind that controls my whole body? Isn't the mind the battlefield on which we encounter the evil one? Wouldn't all of us have appreciated being born with a special mind such as Christ had?

If we can admit that Jesus was *not* like us on this crucial point, then it would be clearly ludicrous to maintain that He came exactly like us. As Knight noted, Jones was "forced to admit that Jesus had 'precisely our nature' only in terms of His flesh. He did not have our passions, because He did not have the fallen mind of Adam and Eve." When it was all said and done, therefore, Knight observed, "Jones demonstrated that there was more than 'a particle of difference' between Christ and other human beings" (*From 1888 to Apostasy*, p. 139).

Regardless of all this, many modern followers of Jones and Waggoner prefer to cling to Jones's ringing declaration that there was "not a particle of difference" between Jesus' nature and ours.

This, then, is the theological legacy of Jones and Waggoner. To many of their modern followers they are larger than life, and nothing must eclipse the light that shines from them.

Why M. L. Andreasen did not more openly flaunt his connection with these two luminaries is not quite clear to me. Perhaps it had something to do with their pariah status toward the end of their lives—the very time when Andreasen was beginning to rise in the church. But there could be no doubt that the fundamental aspects of Andreasen's theology comport with those of Jones and Waggoner.

In his own right, however, Andreasen has played a major role in the thinking of many today. We now turn to his contribution.

---

[1] George R. Knight, *From 1888 to Apostasy: The Case of A. T. Jones* (Washington, D.C., and Hagerstown, Md.: Review and Herald Pub. Assn., 1987).

[2] Compare Robert J. Wieland and Donald K. Short, *1888 Re-examined* (Meadow Vista, Calif.: The 1888 Message Study Committee, 1987), p. 118.

[3] Compare Arnold Wallenkampf, *What Every Adventist Should Know About 1888* (Hagerstown, Md.: Review and Herald Pub. Assn., 1988), p. 18; Knight, *From 1888 to Apostasy*, p. 70.

[4] See E. G. White, "Letter to Eli Curtis," *A Word to the "Little Flock,"* p. 12. She indicated that she felt "fully authorized by the Lord" to recommend Crosier's article "to every saint." Crosier's article appeared in the *Day-Star Extra*, Feb. 7, 1846.

Chapter 3

LOCKED IN BITTER CONFLICT:
Andreasen Versus
the Brethren

A s we have seen, the perfectionist agitation within the Seventh-day Adventist Church today had its genesis in the post-1888 teachings of A. T. Jones and E. J. Waggoner. In this chapter I wish to show that *the linkage of sanctification, perfection, and Christ's nature* that has become dominant among certain groups in Adventism today is a direct legacy of M. L. Andreasen's theology.

Milian Lauritz Andreasen was born in Denmark in 1876. He joined the Adventist Church as a teenager, not long after migrating to the United States in 1894 (from Canada, where he first landed in 1890). After working for a brief period as an elementary school teacher, he became a minister and was ordained in the early 1900s. Throughout the years he held various church portfolios, among them: president of Hutchinson Theological Seminary—essentially a foreign language Adventist school for Scandinavian workers in Minnesota (1910-1918); president of Union College in Nebraska (1931-1938); professor of theology at the SDA Theological Seminary, then located in Washington, D. C. (1938-1949); and field secretary of the General Conference (1941-1950).

Recognized by church leaders as a leading Bible scholar and theologian, Andreasen was requested on three separate occasions to prepare Sabbath school lessons or lesson helps for the worldwide church. He authored several books and held a lifelong interest in the doctrines of the atonement and the sanctuary.

As a longtime seminary professor, Andreasen touched the lives of a multitude of leaders in the Adventist Church, and many still remember him fondly.

What Shaped Him?

When the now famous General Conference session convened in Minneapolis, Minnesota, in 1888, Andreasen was only 12 years old, still in Europe and not yet an Adventist. But during his formative years as a worker in the Adventist Church in the United States, the aftermath of that session, merging with events taking place in the world, would help shape his theological direction for the rest of his life.

During the decade following 1888, Adventists in the United States were standing on tiptoe in expectation of Jesus' imminent return. All around the country and in the world in general, they thought they saw signs of the nearness of Christ's coming. Especially were they impressed by developments in the area of Sunday legislation in connection with the Blair amendment to the U.S. Constitution, which was making its way through the U.S. Congress. Many, including Ellen White herself, had the deep conviction that "the loud cry" of Revelation 18:1, 2 had already begun and that the time of trouble could be just ahead.

But the nineties passed, and the Lord did not return.

During the first decade of the twentieth century, the attention of Adventist leaders was largely taken up with administrative problems—especially of reorganization and realignment. They were also distracted by certain theological problems such as pantheism and the "holy flesh" movement.

But as the church entered the second decade, especially after the beginning of World War I in 1914, it was swept by another wave of Second Coming expectation. The period saw heated discussions and debates over questions of Bible prophecy—in particular, the identity of the "king of the north" and the nature of the battle of Armageddon—the so-called Eastern question. Many saw in World War I the fulfillment of Revelation 16:16: "And he gathered them together into a place called in the Hebrew tongue, Armageddon." And if this were, indeed, the battle of Armageddon, then, of course, Christ's coming was just around the corner. The fall of Turkey in 1918 fueled the prevailing speculations. So preoccupied had many people become with these questions that church leaders found it necessary to call for a return to an emphasis on righteousness by faith such as was evidenced at the 1888 General Conference session in Minneapolis.

What is significant here is that this happened to be the period in which Andreasen was coming into prominence as an Adventist leader. Apparently, he did not participate in these speculations, if we might judge from his reaction to a similar wave of expectation surrounding World War II. In a 1942 report to the General Conference officers, he lamented that "the vital doctrine of the 144,000 . . . had ceased to be preached," having been replaced by "fantastic theories in regard to the [Second World] War, Hitler, and the future." In that same report he also complained about widespread discussion and debate among our people over the subject of Armageddon (Andreasen to J. L. McElhany and W. H. Branson, Dec. 25, 1942, p. 5).

I made the point in my 1981 book about the sanctuary that Andreasen's theology developed against the background of these controversies and was shaped by them. It is true that he despised the fantastic speculations in regard to the Parousia, but I think it was impossible for him to ignore them. Their manifest failure must have impressed him, leading him to articulate a theological reason for the delay. That reason would come to center on "the vital doctrine of the 144,000," obtusely referred to in that 1942 report to the General Conference leaders.

In my judgment, the perception of a delay of the Parousia lies at the heart of the controversy over righteousness by faith and perfection in our church at the present time. And my thesis is that the single most important spark for the contemporary agitation on this question has sprung from the theology of M. L. Andreasen. I will present now a brief outline of Andreasen's position on the atonement and then move on in the following section to his teaching about Christ's human nature. The one leads into the other, you see. Then I will attempt to show how these ideas connect with the notion of the absolute perfection of a final remnant—the 144,000—and how that perfection relates to the apparent delay of the Second Coming.

Andreasen on the Atonement

Perhaps in no other place did Andreasen outline his position on the atonement more clearly than in his commentary on the book of Hebrews. And perhaps the cardinal text that provided the basis for his thinking on this question was, surprisingly, Hebrews 1:3: "Who being the brightness of his glory, and the express image of his person, and upholding all things by the word of his power, *when he had by himself purged our sins, sat down on the right hand of the Majesty on high.*"

For most of us, the basic meaning of the italicized words is clear: After Christ had, by His death, taken care of sin, after He had done what needed doing about this cosmic malady, He went back to the throne of God in heaven. As the New International Version puts it: "After he had provided purification for sins, he sat down at the right hand of the Majesty in heaven."

But Andreasen found deep theological subtleties buried in that single text. "The phrase 'purification of sins' [a rendering Andreasen preferred over the KJV's 'purged our sins']" wrote Andreasen, "in the Greek is in the middle voice." "[Thus], when Christ is said to have made 'purification of sins,' its first meaning is that this refers to and reacts upon Himself." That is to say "in His own life He overcame temptation" (M. L. Andreasen, *The Book of Hebrews*, p. 53).

With this single text as a basis, then, Andreasen divided the atonement into three phases. The *first* phase comprehends Christ's life and ministry, during which He made an end of sin. According to Andreasen, this involved the "complete eradication of sin out of the life"—that is, Christ's own life. "It means sanctification, the uprooting of every evil" (*ibid.*, p. 54). Bear in mind that according to Andreasen, all this was accomplished in *Christ's own person* during His earthly life. Christ demonstrated, argued Andreasen, that sin could be wholly overcome and that complete victory was possible. This part of His work He finished before the cross (see Roy Adams, *The Sanctuary Doctrine*, p. 204).

The *second* phase of the atonement, a brief period according to Andreasen, began in Gethsemane and was completed on the cross. It comprehends Christ's sacrifice for the sins of the world. Here on the cross He bore the curse, took the transgressor's place, and paid the penalty (see *The Sanctuary Doctrine*, p. 205).

For Andreasen, the *third* phase of the atonement embraces Christ's session in the heavenly sanctuary and involves the demonstration that He must make in His saints on earth. In that demonstration Christ must show that His complete victory over sin was not a unique phenomenon, but rather is repeatable in His end-time saints. When this demonstration has been accomplished in the experience of the 144,000, *then* Christ will come to claim them as His own (*Hebrews*, pp. 58, 59).

Before the Parousia can occur, therefore, it is necessary for the saints to prove that they can be "completely victorious over sin." This process of eliminating and destroying sin in the last-day saints, the 144,000, is part of the cleansing of the sanctuary (*ibid.*, pp. 58-60).

So, then, two points stand out in Andreasen's atonement theology: *First*, Christ gained access into the holy place of the heavenly sanctuary *only after* He had made purification for sins, which, according to Andreasen's interpretation of Hebrews 1:3, means that Christ conquered sin, eliminating it *from His own life* (*ibid.*, p. 59). (Note that Andreasen's own expression was "eliminating . . . [sin] from *the life*"—almost as if afraid to come out clearly with the crass assertion. But the context makes it clear what he means.)

Later Andreasen would return to Christ's accomplishment during the first phase of the atonement as His passport for entrance into the presence of the Father. "And when His work was done, He presented Himself before God for acceptance. The body given Him of God; the body in which He conquered temptation and gained complete victory; . . . *the body cleansed and purified from every defilement*; . . . the cleansed, holy, sanctified, consecrated body in which God's ideal for man was at last realized—this body Christ presents before the Father, and the Father accepts it, and through it He gains entrance" (*ibid.*, p. 443; italics supplied).

If you do not immediately grasp the theological precariousness of the foregoing statement, just remember that the *mind is an essential part of the human body*, whether Andreasen consciously realized this or not. Which means that Christ's mind, with the rest of His body, needed cleansing. This removes the discussion from the realm of "benign" (or simply physical) impurity to that of the malignant pollution of the very heart of Christ's person.

Now with that as a background, read Andreasen's statement again, and consider its enormous implications for the integrity of our Saviour. To put it bluntly, if Andreasen's statement is correct, *then technically we do not have a Saviour,* because how could the Saviour Himself stand in need of spiritual cleansing?

But what all this means for Andreasen is that our bodies (including our minds, of course) need to undergo a similar cleansing, a similar purification, if we are ever to gain entrance into the Father's presence.

This brings us to the *second* pillar of Andreasen's atonement theology—namely, that Christ's victory over sin during the first phase of the atonement was not unique but is to be repeated in the end-time saints.

Reason for the Delay

So why had the Parousia not occurred in the 1890s? Why had it not occurred in connection with World War I? Or in connection with World War II? The reason, Andreasen would say, was that the remnant had not yet achieved the standard of perfection that God required. They had not yet reached the state of absolute sinlessness.

Absolute perfection? Absolute sinlessness? Indeed! That's what Andreasen taught.

No, we do not reach that stage in a day, just as "the fruit of a tree is not perfected in a day." The perfection seen at each stage of the fruit's development Andreasen would term "relative perfection"—the perfection that Paul referred to when he admonished, "Let us therefore, as many as be perfect, be thus minded" (Phil. 3:15) (see *The Book of Hebrews,* pp. 466, 467).

But, noted Andreasen, Paul himself admitted in Philippians 3:12 that he had not yet attained to absolute perfection. "He does not claim absolute perfection, which is equivalent to holiness" (*ibid.,* p. 467).

But "will any ever attain to the perfection to which Paul said he had not attained?" queried Andreasen. His own answer, though circuitous, is nevertheless clear. "We should be disappointed if Paul had claimed absolute perfection; for no man who attains to this will ever claim it, or perhaps know it. God knows, but [the] man himself will make no such claim.

"But will any ever reach that stage? We believe so. Read the description of the 144,000 in Revelation 14:5: '. . . And in their mouth was found no guile: for they are without fault before the throne of God'" (*ibid.*, pp. 467, 468; italics supplied).

Andreasen believed that this will be the group living just before Jesus comes and who will have attained to absolute perfection, or holiness (*ibid.*, p. 468).

This line of thought has proven very attractive to certain ones among us. I have taken the time to follow it through in the thinking of its proponents, and I have noticed the subtle legalism that undergirds it.

Follow Andreasen, for example, as he developed the concept of sanctification that leads ultimately to "absolute perfection." The path of holiness, he stated, is sometimes slow and painstaking. We must struggle against "intoxicants and tobacco" and other such evils. But we must take them one at a time. "Only when he [the Christian] has successfully disposed of one enemy is he ready for another" (*ibid.*, p. 465).

And what is the benefit of all this striving? Said Andreasen: "The man who resists unto blood, striving against sin, *will receive due credit for his attainment*" (*ibid.*; italics supplied).[1]

Then follows this incredible statement: "As we thus walk along the way of sanctification, meeting one problem after another as it comes to us, we are progressing in sanctification and *nearing the goal of holiness.* From the moment we start, God is imputing righteousness to us. We are indeed not perfected, but we are headed in the right direction, *and should we die before we reach the goal, God will adjudge our motives and give us credit for what we would have done had we had the opportunity*" (*ibid.*, p. 466; italics supplied).

"God will . . . give us credit for what we would have done." Can you see where this kind of theology leads?

Andreasen had written all this before 1948, but no one seemed to notice, and few would have taken issue with him even if they did. He was, after all, the recognized authority in the church on the question of the sanctuary and the atonement. However, events commencing in the mid-fifties were to change all this, and Andreasen would find himself in deep controversy with church leaders—a controversy that would bring into the open the other fundamental leg of his theology: his concept of Christ's human nature. This is the central focus of what follows.

Adventist-Evangelical Conversations Spark Bitter Conflict

In March 1955 four prominent Adventist leaders commenced a series of official conversations with certain evangelical leaders. It would plunge the church into controversy for decades.

The evangelicals involved were Walter R. Martin, George E. Cannon, and later Donald G. Barnhouse. Martin, a Southern Baptist clergyman, was a Ph.D. candidate at New York University, researching for a dissertation on the subject "Non-Christian Religions in the United States." A research polemicist, he was preparing a book against Seventh-day Adventists and wanted to ascertain, as accurately as possible, what we really believed and taught. George Cannon was a professor of theology on the faculty of Nyack Missionary College in New York. Donald Barnhouse was then a popular radio preacher in Philadelphia, pastor of a large Presbyterian church in the same city, and editor in chief of *Eternity* magazine.

The Adventist Church was represented by LeRoy Edwin Froom, W. E. Read, T. E. Unruh, and later Roy Allan Anderson, then editor of *Ministry*.

The purpose of the conversations was to provide evangelical church leaders with an accurate account of the distinctive beliefs of Seventh-day Adventists. The group met in the Takoma Park offices of the General Conference throughout a period of a year or more.

Andreasen took a dim view of these conversations. To him, they represented a capitulation—a sellout—on the part of Adventist Church leadership. A confrontation quickly developed between him and high-ranking Adventist leaders, particularly the then president of the General Conference, Reuben R. Figuhr, with whom

Andreasen exchanged a series of strongly worded letters, especially during the period of February to December 1957.

As the conflict grew, Andreasen came to see himself as the target of suppression on the part of the church's leadership.[2] In the midst of the controversy his credentials were suspended by a General Conference Officers and Union Presidents Council in April 1961. In the minutes Andreasen was accused of making "grave and false charges against the leadership" of the Seventh-day Adventist Church. The minutes argued that to permit ministers to retain credentials while continuing to engage in active controversy with the duly constituted leadership would produce only increasing confusion in the minds of the people. According to the minutes, the vote was unanimous, but taken in hope that the suspension would not be permanent (see "Suspension of Credentials of M. L. Andreasen," Minutes, General Conference Officers and Union Presidents Council, Apr. 6, 1958, p. 9).

Andreasen reacted sharply to the General Conference action, declaring it "illegal and void." He called for the impeachment of the General Conference president and predicted a great shaking among church leaders because of the suspension.

Why the Strong Reaction?

Almost certainly one reason for Andreasen's reaction was that he had not been consulted. How could our leaders fail to invite him to participate in such delicate and high-level conversations, involving subjects on which he had always been regarded as the recognized, undisputed authority in the church? To Andreasen and others who knew and respected him, that was simply unthinkable.

And why, indeed, was he not invited? Arthur White in a personal conversation with me years ago suggested a plausible reason: Andreasen by that time was not only retired (he had retired in 1950 and these meetings took place in 1955), but he was also well advanced in years—nearly 80.

Another possible reason (suggested by Andreasen biographer Virginia Steinweg) centers on a dispute between Andreasen and the brethren over Sabbath school materials. According to Steinweg,

Andreasen had been asked by the General Conference Sabbath School Department to revise his three-volume commentary, *Isaiah, the Gospel Prophet*, in connection with the Sabbath school lessons for the first two quarters of 1957. These Sabbath school lesson helps, of course, are prepared long in advance—in Andreasen's case, well before 1955. However, because of a change in both personnel and policy, Andreasen's book was no longer needed—and this after he had gone to considerable time and effort to prepare a new manuscript.

As a matter of principle, Andreasen demanded reimbursement to the tune of $3,000—a considerable sum of money in the early 1950s, perhaps equivalent to no less than $25,000 in today's economy. Steinweg believes that hard feelings generated by this unhappy incident could have played a role in discouraging the brethren from inviting Andreasen's participation in these conversations (see Virginia Steinweg, *Without Fear or Favor: The Life of M. L. Andreasen*, pp. 171, 173).

Whatever the cause, the fact is that Andreasen was not consulted. And it would be reasonable to conclude that he felt slighted. But I think we need to go one step further if we are to understand the full extent of his anger against church leaders. When we do that, we will discover that the basic reason for his irritation was theological.

So far as Andreasen was concerned, the leaders of the church were bent on a course that compromised the very essence, the very foundation, of Seventh-day Adventism—namely, the *doctrines of Christ's human nature and the atonement*. In his theology these two were closely connected. We have already looked at his position on the atonement. Let's now briefly notice what he taught on the human nature of Christ.

Andreasen on Christ's Human Nature
Barnhouse, a participant in the SDA-evangelical dialogues, commenting on the Adventist position vis-à-vis Christ's human nature, reported that they had affirmed that His nature was "sinless, holy, and perfect." Moreover, they asserted, said Barnhouse, that any other position was "completely repugnant" to them (D. G. Barnhouse, "Are Seventh-day Adventists Christians?" *Eternity*, vol. 7, 1956, p. 6).

Andreasen was outraged!

Nor did the situation improve with the publication of the book *Questions on Doctrine*.[3] With the publication of that work Andreasen's anger rose to new heights, and his contempt for Adventist leaders took a quantum leap. Published in the wake and as a result of the SDA-evangelical dialogues, *Questions on Doctrine* was designed to share with a wider audience—both inside and outside Adventism— the position of Adventists on fundamental questions put forward by Walter Martin and his group.

One statement, among others, that stirred Andreasen's ire appears on page 383 of *Questions on Doctrine*. "He could rightly be 'chosen out of the people' because He was 'holy, harmless, undefiled, separate from sinners' (Heb. 7:26). He came into humanity, not by natural generation, but by a miracle. His birth was supernatural; God was His Father. Although born in the flesh, He was nevertheless God, and was exempt from the inherited passions and pollutions that corrupt the natural descendants of Adam. He was 'without sin,' not only in His outward conduct, but in His very nature. He could truly say, 'the prince of this world cometh, and hath nothing [or 'findeth no response'] in me' (John 14:30). There was nothing in Him that responded to the evil one. And just such a priest we needed. Had He been defiled by even the taint of sin, He would have been disqualified from being either our sacrifice or our High Priest. But though sinless in His life and in His nature, He was nevertheless 'in all points tempted like as we are, yet without sin' (Heb. 4:15). And because of that, He is able to sympathize with us in every sorrow or trial."

Andreasen was aghast! Scandalized!

What, then, was his conception of Christ's human nature? And how important was this for the fundamental emphasis of his theology? Here we come to the heart of the issue.

As Andreasen understood it, Christ in His incarnation took upon Himself sinful human nature. He was not, as *Questions on Doctrine* had affirmed, "exempt from the inherited passions and pollutions that corrupt the descendants of Adam." For Andreasen, the position of these leaders amounted to nothing short of heresy, and he called it so (see Andreasen, *Letters to the Churches*, Series A, No. 1, "The Incarnation. Was Christ Exempt?" p. 8).

Andreasen reasoned that the original charge leveled by the devil was that obedience to the moral law, the Ten Commandments, was impossible for finite beings. Thus Christ became finite and incarnate to demonstrate that human beings can indeed keep the law and gain the victory over every sin. Therefore to exempt from "inherited passions and pollutions" the very One who came to demonstrate that God's law could be perfectly kept would constitute an act of deception—an act of fraud. This would automatically invalidate Christ's role as our example because, argued Andreasen, "one who has not struggled with passions can have no understanding of their power," nor can He have "the joy of overcoming them" (*ibid.*, p. 7).

Accordingly, Andreasen referred to the position taken by *Questions on Doctrine* as the "acme of all heresy." He feared that the position of the Adventist leaders, if accepted, would destroy all true religion and completely nullify the plan of salvation (*ibid.*, pp. 7, 8).

He demanded a hearing by the General Conference—a hearing complete with stenographers and/or tape recorders, a public hearing—in which he could put forward his position and refute the dangerous teachings being foisted upon the people of God (see Andreasen *Letters*, Series A, No. 5, "Why Not a Hearing?" p. 4). The brethren, for their part, agreed to a hearing, but with no stenographers or tape recorders. The group would simply select one from among its number to take notes and prepare a summary of the issues and questions discussed. After many letters back and forth between Andreasen and Figuhr on the question, negotiations broke down (*ibid.*, pp. 5ff).

To Andreasen, the position of the brethren was completely unacceptable. It amounted to a denial of a hearing. And thus he felt compelled to take his case directly to the people in a series of papers that he entitled *Letters to the Churches*.

I want to share some excerpts from these *Letters* in order to highlight further Andreasen's position on the human nature of Christ. If we keep in mind his discussion of Christ's accomplishments during the first phase of the atonement (covered earlier in this chapter), then we can understand the reason for his strong emphasis on Christ's affinity to us. He must be *exactly* like us if we would ever be required to do what He did during the first phase of the atonement. If He were not 100 percent like us—*in every way*—then we are at a disadvantage (in comparison with Him) in our striving toward absolute perfection.

With this background, we are ready to follow the distinguished professor in his radical articulation of Christ's identity with us. The excerpts included are given without any emphasis of my own (so as to keep Andreasen's own emphases unconfused). Neither do I offer any explanatory comments. I simply want Andreasen's own thinking to stand out. Every sentence has weight in defining the contours of his position on Christ's human nature.

Excerpts From the Letters

"The other word to which we would call attention is *behoved*. Speaking of Christ, Paul says, 'in all things it behoved him to be made like unto his brethren, that he might be a merciful and faithful high priest in things pertaining to God, to make reconciliation for the sins of the people' (Heb. 2:17). While *became* in verse 10 is a mild word, *behoved* in verse 17 (*ophilo* in Greek) is a strong word and is defined 'under obligation,' 'ought,' 'must,' 'should,' 'bound,' 'indebted,' 'duty,' 'owe.' If Christ is to be a merciful and faithful high priest, Paul says it behooves Him 'in all things' to be like His brethren. This is obligatory. It is a duty He owes and must not avoid. He cannot make reconciliation for men unless He takes His place with them and in all things becomes like them. It is not a question of choice. He *should*, He *must*, He *ought* to, He is *under obligation* to, He *owes* it. . . . One who has never been weak and sick, who has never struggled with temptations, is unable fully to sympathize with those who are thus afflicted" (Series A, No. 1, "The Incarnation. Was Christ Exempt?" [1959], p. 3).[4]

"With these reflections in mind, we read with astonishment and perplexity, mingled with sorrow, the false statement in *Questions on Doctrine*, page 383, that Christ was 'exempt from the inherited passions and pollutions that corrupt the natural descendants of Adam'" (*ibid.*, p. 4).

"Passion is defined: 'Originally suffering or agony (*sic*) . . . any of the emotions as hate, grief, love, fear, joy. . . . Passion usually implies a strong emotion that has an overpowering or compelling effect.' Passion is an inclusive word. While originally it has reference to sorrow, suffering, agony, it is not confined to these meanings nor to passions of the flesh only, but includes all man's emotions as mentioned above, as well as anger, sorrow, hunger, pity; it includes, in fact, all temptations that incite men to action. To take these emotions away from a man, to exempt him from all temptation, results in a creature less than a man, a kind of no-man, a shadow man, a non-entity, which Markham calls 'brother to the ox'" (*ibid.*, pp. 4, 5).

"If Christ was exempt from the passions of mankind, He was different from other men, none of whom is so exempt. Such teaching is tragic, and completely contrary to what Seventh-day Adventists have always taught and believed" (*ibid.*, p. 5).

"If Christ had been exempt from passions, He would have been unable to understand or help mankind. It, therefore, behooved Him 'in all things . . . to be made like unto his brethren, that he might be a merciful and faithful high priest. . . . For in that he himself hath suffered being tempted, he is able to succour them that are tempted' (Heb. 2:17, 18). A Saviour who has never been tempted, never has had to battle with passions, who has never 'offered up prayers and supplications with strong crying and tears unto him who was able to save him from death,' who 'though he were a son' never learned obedience by the things He suffered, but was 'exempt' from the very things that a true Saviour must experience; such a saviour is what this new theology offers us. It is not the kind of Saviour I need, nor the world. One who has never struggled with passions can have no understanding of their power, nor has He ever had the joy of overcoming them. If God extended special favors and exemptions to Christ, in that very act He disqualified Him for His work. There can be no heresy more harmful than that here discussed. It takes away the Saviour I have known and substitutes for Him a weak personality, not considered by God capable of resisting and conquering the passions which He asks men to overcome" (*ibid.*, p. 7).

"Only as Christ placed Himself on the level of the humanity He had come to save could He demonstrate to men how to overcome their infirmities and passions. If the men with whom He associated had understood that He was *exempt* from the passions with which they had to battle, His influence would immediately have been destroyed and He would be reckoned a deceiver. His pronouncement, 'I have overcome the world' (John 16:33), would be accepted as a dishonest boast; for without passions He had nothing to overcome" (*ibid.*, p. 8).

"That God exempted Christ from the passions that corrupt men is the acme of heresy. It is destruction of all true religion and completely nullifies the plan of redemption, and makes God a deceiver and Christ His accomplice" (*ibid.*).

"*Questions on Doctrine*, page 383, states that Christ was exempt. The Spirit of Prophecy makes clear that Christ was *not exempt* from the temptations and passions that afflict men. Whoever accepts the new theology must reject the *Testimonies*. There is no other choice" (*ibid.*, p. 13).

"This [the SDA conversations with the evangelicals] is a most interesting and dangerous situation. As one official who was not in favor of what was being done stated to me: 'We are being sold down the river.' What a sight for heaven and earth! The church of the living God which has been given the commission to preach the gospel to every creature under heaven and call men to come out of Babylon is now standing at the door of these churches asking permission to enter and become one of them. How are the mighty fallen! Had their plan succeeded, we might now be a member of some evangelical association and not a distinctive Seventh-day Adventist church anymore, in secrecy 'sold down the river.' This is more than apostasy. This is giving up Adventism. It is the rape of a whole people. It is denying God's leading in the past" (Series A, No. 6, "The Atonement," p. 7).

In Reflection

These are not mild words. And they explain the dogged persistence of Andreasen's modern disciples. Although the brethren prevailed administratively against Andreasen, the embattled retired professor was able to kick up enough fuss to ensure that *Questions on*

Doctrine would not go into reprint. Today the book is out of print, and I get the impression that few of our leaders have the courage, even now, to defend it publicly.

Earlier I promised to lay out the statements by Andreasen without comment. And I did. But lest anyone misunderstand my silence here, let me give one example of the character of some of his bold assertions. I will do this by repeating just one of his statements and following it up with one from Ellen G. White. (Remember that the emphases in Andreasen's statement will be his own.)

Andreasen: "*Questions on Doctrine* . . . states that Christ was exempt. The Spirit of Prophecy makes clear that Christ was *not exempt* from temptations and passions that afflict men. Whoever accepts the new theology must reject the *Testimonies*. There is no other choice" (*Letters*, Series A, No. 1, "The Incarnation. Was Christ Exempt?" p. 3).

Ellen G. White: "He is a brother in our infirmities, *but not in possessing like passions*" (*Testimonies*, vol. 2, p. 202; italics supplied).

I remember how I felt years ago when I saw this discrepancy and scores of others in Andreasen's writings. Immersed in my dissertation on the sanctuary, things were more vivid to me then. I'd had conversations with people who had known Andreasen as a friend or had been taught by him. And I could sense the affection and respect some still had for this Adventist giant of yesteryear.

Yet the picture of the man that I was finding in the *Letters* was so different, so pathetic. Writing to Figuhr, Andreasen had affirmed his allegiance and loyalty to Ellen White's writings. "In my more than sixty years of official connection with the denomination, one of my chief aims has been to inspire confidence in the Spirit of prophecy. *The last two years I have spoken on the subject 204 times*" (*Letters*, Series A, No. 4, "A Résumé," p. 9).

How could such a self-confessed expert in Ellen G. White's writings have missed such a clear-cut published statement on a topic in which he had such a vital interest? Or—the thought caused me pain—was he, in fact, fully aware of its existence? Today his modern disciples, unable to ignore that statement (and a host of others in a similar vein), have come up with some ingenious theological gymnastics to get around it,[5] but Andreasen didn't do that. Did he deliberately choose to ignore Ellen White's statement? Or worse yet, did he choose to ride headlong into its face, stirring up widespread confusion in the church in the name of the very one whose words he'd chosen to set aside?

However, with this and other instances of manipulation of the evidence before me, I spent long, pensive moments at my dissertation desk as I contemplated what this might signify for the character of a saint of God facing the closing days of his life. Was this the kind of integrity I should expect? What went wrong? But we must leave all this in the hands of the Lord, our merciful Saviour.

The last days of Andreasen were sad indeed. As the theological conflict deepened, other problems arose, including that of his second wife's eligibility for General Conference retirement benefits. The situation deteriorated to the extent that he threatened legal action when the church began to show some reluctance to pay his sustentation allowance on account of his intense agitation (Andreasen, "Shooting the Watchdog," unpublished paper, n.d., p. 2). In a state of deep grief, close to depression, Andreasen took to writing letters to God. He developed a duodenal ulcer, which eventually hemorrhaged, ending his life.

When I was writing my 1981 book on the sanctuary, I found among the Andreasen papers in the E. G. White Research Center at Andrews University an undated document addressed "To Whom It May Concern." The document alleged that, just before his death, Andreasen made reconciliation with General Conference president R. R. Figuhr in a mood of "brotherly love." At this meeting, according to the document, "Andreasen indicated his regrets over the estrangement between himself and the brethren."

An identical copy of this document at the Ellen G. White Estate office at the General Conference headquarters in Silver Spring, Maryland, carries the name of D. A. Delafield, a former trustee of the E. G. White Estate. However, in a personal interview with me in August 1979, Delafield could not remember preparing the document. The late Arthur White, another former trustee, characterized the whole affair to me as a deathbed confession.

Thus Andreasen's final attitude toward the controversy with church leaders remains murky. But I would assume from Arthur White's response just cited that, whatever one might think of it, something did take place. And Andreasen biographer Virginia Steinweg seems to support a kind of reconciliation in the end (see Virginia Steinweg, *Without Fear*, p. 181; T. E. Unruh, "The Seventh-day Adventist-Evangelical Conferences of 1955-1956," p. 45).

But regardless of what actually happened, an atmosphere of pathos and tragedy surrounds Andreasen's sunset years. He died a pathetic figure.

When I reflect on all this, against the background of the glaring contradictions and misrepresentations that I find in his *Letters to the Churches*, I have difficulty seeing in Andreasen anything resembling the portrait of the absolutely perfect ones whom he taught will comprise earth's final generation of Christians. But, if I am faithful, I expect to see Brother Andreasen in heaven—even though I believe that his theology, however firmly he himself believed it, was misguided and wrongheaded. And I believe that the merciful Saviour to whom he had dedicated his whole life will not hold it against him.

In the next chapter, I want to examine the question of Christ's human nature, the basic focus of Andreasen's theology and that of his contemporary supporters.

---

[1] After decades of the church's emphasis on righteousness by faith, many of Andreasen's modern followers have wised up in their use of language. But every so often the legalistic foundation of their theology surfaces, as in the following statement by Ron Spear: "But by His [Christ's] perfect obedience to the law, He would open the way for fallen man *to be redeemed by following His example in perfect lawkeeping* by the power of the Holy Spirit working successfully in the life to keep man from sin" ("The New Theology: A False Gospel," *Our Firm Foundation*, March 1993, p. 12; italics supplied).

[2] I document this in *The Sanctuary Doctrine*, p. 175, footnote.

[3] *Questions on Doctrine* was prepared by a representative group of SDA leaders, Bible teachers, and editors.

[4] In the context of this discussion, nonexemption (in the eyes both of Andreasen and his opponents) is equivalent to possession. That is to say, if Christ was not exempt from passions, He did possess them. And the argument that He did not possess evil human passion means that He was exempt from them.

[5] See for example, Larson, *The Word Was Made Flesh*, pp. 22-26.

Chapter 4

THE WORD BECAME FLESH:
Like Adam or
Like Us?

Years ago I attended Sabbath school at a Brooklyn, New York, church. The lesson study, taken on a whole, as we say, was proceeding smoothly under the able direction of two ministerial students from Andrews University.

In the midst of this tranquillity, one brother suddenly rose to his feet and, perhaps with mischief aforethought, made this startling pronouncement: "I believe," he said, "that Jesus Christ was born in sin and shapen in iniquity," using a popular variation of Psalm 51:5.

As he sat down (and he never spoke again), hands went up everywhere. The whole place lit up with emotion. Somehow, instinctively, the people knew that something was suspect about this brother's assertion. They seemed to know that everyone born that way needs a Saviour. It is an issue that has captured Christian reflection and controversy for many centuries.

Hence the question before us: Like Adam or like us? Which was it?

The Mystery of Jesus

In typical Eastern style, Nicodemus began his nocturnal interview with Jesus with a mouthful of compliments: "Rabbi, we know that thou art a teacher come from God: for no man can do these miracles . . ."

Jesus gently brushed aside the flatteries and went directly to the point: "Except a man be born again, he cannot see the kingdom of God" (John 3:1-3).

Attempting to avoid the spiritual thrust of Jesus' remark,

Nicodemus posed a conundrum: "How can a man be born when he is old? can he enter the second time into his mother's womb, and be born?" (verse 4). That question is important for the subject before us because it brings into sharp focus, albeit indirectly and inadvertently, the miracle and mystery of the Incarnation. Nicodemus probably did not realize that he was seated in the presence of One who was Himself a living specimen of an infinitely more complex phenomenon. Jesus was the One whom Micah described when he told of a person "whose goings forth have been from of old, from everlasting" (Micah 5:2). He was the One described by Isaiah as "The mighty God, The everlasting Father" (Isa. 9:6).

And the astonishing claim of the New Testament is that this very Person did, in fact, enter the womb of a human mother — a *part of His own creation* — developed for nine months as a regular embryo would, and then emerged as a helpless, screaming baby in a Bethlehem stable. Absolutely mind-boggling! Said Ellen White: "When we want a deep problem to study, let us fix our minds on the most marvelous thing that ever took place in earth or heaven — the incarnation of the Son of God" (*The SDA Bible Commentary*, Ellen G. White Comments, vol. 7, p. 904). The English word "incarnation" comes from two Latin words: *in* (meaning "in") and *caro* or *carnis* (meaning "flesh"). Thus, "incarnation" means literally "in flesh" or, in reference to Christ, "becoming flesh."

In Scripture the clearest affirmation of this doctrine is found in John 1:14: "And the Word was made flesh, and dwelt among us, (and we beheld his glory, the glory as of the only begotten of the Father,) full of grace and truth."

The Incarnation is the key doctrine of Christianity, the central doctrine of the Christian faith. Without it the whole canon of Scripture becomes a meaningless document — a *non-sense*. Yet many Christians throughout the centuries have had difficulty accepting the idea of the Incarnation. Some, like the Gnostics, could not bring themselves to accept Jesus' *real humanity*. Others, like the Ebionites (an early group of Jewish Christians), could not accept the Saviour's *real divinity*. The initial debate and controversy that ensued from these conflicting views of Christ were intense and bitter and lasted 300 years—until the Council of Nicea in A.D. 325. Delegates to that council, representing all Christendom, finally came to an agreement on the question of the Saviour's divinity and humanity. I quote from the Nicene Creed: "We believe in one God, the Father almighty, . . . and in one Lord, Jesus Christ, . . . Only begotten, that is from the substance of the Father, God from God . . . begotten, not made, of one substance [*homoousios*] with the Father, through Whom all things came into being. . . .

"Who because of us men and because of our salvation came down and became incarnate, becoming man, suffered and rose again on the third day, ascended to the heavens, and will come to judge the living and the dead" (cited in John M. Davidson Kelly, *Early Christian Creeds*, pp. 215, 216).

But if Christ was both God and man, how then were divinity and humanity combined in His person? How did they relate? Was He schizophrenic? Was He one person, or was He two persons? It was an issue of immense theological complexity, and it occupied the attention of theologians and philosophers for another 125 years— until it was settled at the Council of Chalcedon in A.D. 451.

Here is the statement, or at least part of it, which resulted from that council. Notice the extreme caution of the language pressed into the service of this great mystery. Observe the care taken to plug every loophole and thread a way through the theological pitfalls that have bedeviled many through the centuries. It is a ringing testimony to reverent and careful scholarship.

"Following, then, the holy Fathers [that is, the apostles and early Church Fathers], we all with one voice teach . . . that our Lord Jesus Christ is one and the same God, the same perfect in Godhead, the same perfect in manhood, truly God and truly man . . . in all things like unto us, sin only excepted . . . one and the same Christ, Son, Lord, Only begotten, made known in two natures [which exist] without confusion, without change, without division, without separation; the difference of natures having been in no wise taken away by reason of the union, but rather the properties of each being preserved, and [both] concurring into one person . . . not parted or divided into two persons . . . , but one and the same Son and Only-begotten, the divine Logos, the Lord Jesus Christ" (cited in J. Allan Gonzalez, *A History of Christian Thought*, vol. 1, pp. 390, 391).

. In this shining credo, there is a carefully crafted line that highlights an issue on which many to this day have made shipwreck. The line reads: *"In all things like unto us, sin only excepted."*

What does this mean? If Christ did in fact become a human being, how was He able to bypass the universal infection of sin? Was He really like us, or was He like the *unfallen* Adam?

The path before us is strewn with mines and quicksand, and we must thread our way carefully. But in the end, it will be seen that the factor which poses the greatest danger for us is our own hangups and preconceived opinions.

We will look first at the biblical picture and then, because this is a book primarily for Adventists, at the writings of Ellen G. White. Obviously we cannot present every text or quotation on the subject. But nothing essential to the issue will be dodged or swept under the rug. And we will draw our conclusion in the light of the full evidence.

The New Testament Affirmation

Those among us who put forward evidence for Christ's real humanity as though this were a point on which Adventists need to be convinced leave me completely mystified. According to my own observation, most (if not all) Adventists accept fully the fact of Christ's humanity, and there's hardly a need to multiply words in its defense.

But in order not to appear to be negligent on this plank, here in brief is a summary of the evidence—in almost the exact form that all Andrews University seminarians for the past 25 years or so have received it from the lips of longtime theology professor Dr. Raoul Dederen.

1. Jesus is described in the New Testament as possessing the essential elements of human nature—flesh and blood. "Since the children have flesh and blood, he too shared in their humanity so that by his death he might destroy him who holds the power of death" (Heb. 2:14, NIV). And John affirms that "every spirit that acknowledges that Jesus Christ has come in the flesh is from God, but every spirit that does not acknowledge [the humanity of] Jesus is

not from God" (1 John 4:2, 3, NIV).

2. He had a human mother. "But when the time had fully come, God sent his Son, born of a woman, born under law" (Gal. 4:4, NIV).

3. Jesus was subject to the ordinary laws of human development. The Bible says that He "grew in wisdom and stature, and in favor with God and men" (Luke 2:52, NIV; cf. Luke 2:40, 46). The book of Hebrews says that "he learned [came to understand] obedience from what he suffered" (Heb. 5:8, NIV).

4. He experienced physical deficiencies that characterize ordinary human beings. For example, He knew hunger (Matt. 4:2; 21:18), thirst (John 4:7; 19:28), fatigue (Matt. 8:24), and weariness (John 4:6).

So we can have no qualms about the real humanity of Christ — not if we believe the Bible. Speaking about Christ's humiliation, Paul declares that He "made himself nothing, taking the very nature of a servant, being made in human likeness" (Phil 2:7, NIV). And again, in Romans, he affirms that Jesus came "in the likeness of sinful man" (Rom. 8:3, NIV). He came to help us, says the author of Hebrews, and so "for this reason he had to be made like his brothers in every way, in order that he might become a merciful and faithful high priest" (Heb. 2:17, NIV).

It is the height of mischief — not to say dishonesty — to create the impression that the majority of Adventists do not accept the real humanity of the Saviour. Let it be said with all clarity that preachments about Christ's human nature are wasted on most of us. *We believe in it. We preach it. We teach it. Our church would be antichrist not to believe in it.* Can I make it any clearer?

But there is just one "little" exception that some of us have been trying to get across. We will come to it in due course. And that one "little" exception *makes all the difference in the world!*

Ellen G. White Affirms Christ's Humanity

As one turns to the writings of Ellen G. White, one finds a multitude of statements with an emphasis similar to that found in the New Testament. Here is a sampling.

"The humanity of the Son of God is everything to us. It is the golden chain that binds our souls to Christ, and through Christ to God. This is to be our study. Christ was a real man; He gave proof of His humility in becoming a man" (*Selected Messages*, book 1, p. 244).

"By His obedience to all the commandments of God, Christ wrought out a redemption for man. This was not done by going out of Himself to another, but by taking humanity into Himself. . . . Christ took human nature that men might be one with Him as He is one with the Father, that God may love man as He loves His only-begotten Son, that men may be partakers of the divine nature, and be complete in Him" (*The SDA Bible Commentary*, Ellen G. White Comments, vol. 7, p. 927).

"From all eternity Christ was united with the Father, and when He took upon Himself human nature, He was still one with God. He is the link that unites God with humanity" (*Selected Messages*, book 1, p. 228).

"He could not come in the form of an angel; for unless He met man as man, and testified by His connection with God that divine power was not given to Him in a different way to what it will be given to us, He could not be a perfect example for us" (*The SDA Bible Commentary*, Ellen G. White Comments, vol. 7, p. 925).

"Christ ascended to heaven, bearing a sanctified, holy humanity. He took this humanity with Him into the heavenly courts, and through the eternal ages He will bear it, as the One who has redeemed every human being in the City of God" (*ibid.*, vol. 6, p. 1054).

"When Jesus took human nature, and became in fashion as a man, He possessed all the human organism. His necessities were the necessities of a man" (*ibid.*, vol. 5, p. 1130).

"With deep earnestness the mother of Jesus watched the unfolding of His powers. . . . Through the Holy Spirit she received wisdom to cooperate with the heavenly agencies in the development of this child, who could claim only God as His Father" (*The Desire of Ages*, p. 69).

"The Saviour has bound Himself to humanity by a tie that is never to be broken" (*ibid.*, p. 25).

"That He might accomplish His purpose of love for the fallen race, He became bone of our bone and flesh of our flesh. . . .

Divinity and humanity were mysteriously combined, and God and man became one" (*The Faith I Live By*, p. 48).

"In taking upon Himself man's nature in its fallen condition, Christ did not in the least participate in its sin. He was subject to the infirmities and weaknesses by which man is encompassed" (*The SDA Bible Commentary*, Ellen G. White Comments, vol. 5, p. 1131).

"Christ, who knew not the least taint of sin or defilement, took our nature in its deteriorated condition" (*Selected Messages*, book 1, p. 253).

"It would have been an almost infinite humiliation for the Son of God to take man's nature, even when Adam stood in his innocence in Eden. But Jesus accepted humanity when the race had been weakened by four thousand years of sin. Like every child of Adam He accepted the results of the working of the great law of heredity. What these results were is shown in the history of His earthly ancestors. He came with such a heredity to share our sorrows and temptations, and to give us the example of a sinless life" (*The Desire of Ages*, p. 49).

"When Christ bowed His head and died, He bore the pillars of Satan's kingdom with Him to the earth. He vanquished Satan in the same nature over which in Eden Satan obtained the victory. The enemy was overcome by Christ in His human nature. The power of the Saviour's Godhead was hidden. He overcame in human nature, relying upon God for power. This is the privilege of all. In proportion to our faith will be our victory" (*The SDA Bible Commentary*, Ellen G. White Comments, vol. 5, p. 1108).

Powerful statements these—written for our encouragement and consolation. Jesus is truly one with us. He knows what we feel. He understands. And, Ellen G. White informs us, "Christ ascended to heaven, bearing a sanctified, holy humanity," so that "through the eternal ages He will bear it, as the One who has redeemed every human being in the city of God" (*ibid.*, vol. 6, p. 1054).

So Christ's solidarity with us is real and permanent.

These are Adventist statements. We must not dodge them. And *Questions on Doctrine* did not dodge them, contrary to the charges made by Andreasen and his current followers. Get hold of a copy, if you can, and look at pages 653-658. The strongest of the statements

I've included here have been cited there. We do not speak truth if we claim otherwise.

These are good statements. That's what God has done for us. It goes far beyond my most optimistic expectations, and I often find myself wanting to say, "Dear God, You're going too far. Enough that He became like us. But He need not remain like us. I won't mind if He would return to His former state." "But no," God says to me, "His solidarity with the human family is for keeps!"

From Another Angle

Some Adventists, however, have developed a fixation for these affinity statements. Admittedly, they sound so categorical that the novice would never immediately suspect that any mitigating sentiments are possible. But whereas we may easily pardon the novice, we find it simply astonishing that veterans could have the willfulness to draw conclusions from only part of the evidence.

For while it is clear that Jesus shared a very close affinity with us, the evidence also indicates that He was, at the same time, different from us. The book of Hebrews describes Him as "holy, blameless, pure, set apart from sinners" (Heb. 7:26, NIV). And in the words of the apostle John, "In him is no sin" (1 John 3:5). This does not simply mean, as the uninitiated are quick to conclude, that He did not commit sin. It means much more. It means that whereas Psalm 51:5 ("Surely I was sinful at birth, sinful from the time my mother conceived me" [NIV]) applies to every single descendant of Adam, it did *not* apply to Him.

In fact, if we examine carefully the passages in Romans and Philippians that talk about Christ's affinity with us, we will notice something very significant. In the Philippians text, the apostle describes Christ as "taking the very nature [*morphē*] of a servant" (Phil. 2:7, NIV). The word *morphē* is a strong word, used earlier in the very passage to describe Christ's pre-incarnation affinity with the Father. Thus the apostle, most likely, wants to indicate the complete (100 percent) servanthood of Christ.

But when he came to the matter of Christ's ontological affinity with us (that is, Christ's similarity to us in regard to His essential nature and being), Paul changes to a subtler word. He says that Christ was "made in human *likeness*" (Phil. 2:7, NIV), using the Greek word *homoiōmati*. We get a better grasp of this crucial shift when we compare with the parallel text in Romans. There Paul describes Christ as coming "in the likeness [*homoiōmati*] of *sinful* man" (Rom. 8:3).

In their respected lexicon of the New Testament, William Arndt and F. W. Gingrich provide an enlightening insight into the possible reason for the use of this term. They note that the word *homoiōma* (from which *homoiōmati* derives) as used in Romans 8 and Philippians 2 could convey one of two ideas: (1) "That the Lord in his earthly ministry possessed a completely human form and that his physical body was capable of sinning as human bodies are," or (2) "that he had only the form of a man and was looked upon as a human being . . . , whereas in reality he remained a Divine Being even in this world" (*A Greek-English Lexicon of the New Testament and Other Early Christian Literature*, p. 567).

But which, if any, of these possibilities did Paul have in mind? On this question Arndt and Gingrich reached the following conclusion: "In the light of what Paul says about Jesus in general it is safe to assert that his use of our word [*homoiōma*] is to bring out both that Jesus in his earthly career was similar to sinful men and yet not absolutely like them" (*ibid.*).

The validity of this conclusion seems evident from the context of the Romans passage. For there the apostle's concern was to stress how vital was the coming of Jesus to break the hopelessness of our plight in sin. "For what the law was powerless to do *in that it was weakened by the sinful nature*, God did by sending his own Son in the *likeness* of sinful man to be a sin offering" (Rom. 8:3, NIV). Obviously, had Jesus come in our sinful nature—100 percent like us—then "the righteous requirements of the law" (verse 4, NIV) would have remained unfulfilled as always, frustrated by His carnal nature. To express the fact of Christ's affinity and solidarity with us, and at the same time His crucial distinction from us—a distinction that makes all the difference *for* us—Paul carefully employed the subtle Greek word *homoiōma* (likeness).

But someone might question at this point whether I'm forgetting

ORIG. SIN!

some of the passages cited earlier from the book of Hebrews, passages indicating that Jesus was completely like us.

No, I'm not forgetting. The strongest of these passages is "Wherefore *in all things* it behoved him to be made like unto his brethren, that he might be a merciful and faithful high priest" (Heb. 2:17).

We should always be careful not to water down the clear meaning of Scripture or dodge its impact. But neither can we afford to be dogmatic literalists when a text or passage is clearly open to other interpretations. *— such as?*

In this case we have clear, empirical evidence that every person born into the world *immediately* stands in need of redemption. Therefore, if we take a literalist meaning of Hebrews 2:17 and conclude that there is *absolutely* no difference between Christ and ourselves, we will inevitably run up against unsurmountable theological problems, as will become clear later in this chapter.

For now, let us disabuse ourselves of inappropriate literalism by comparing the apparently categorical expression used in Hebrews 2:17 (italicized above) with similar expressions used in other scriptures that we'd hardly want to interpret with the same categoricalness. In Genesis 25:5 Abraham is reported as giving "all that he had" to Isaac. Yet in the very next verse, we find him giving gifts to the sons of his concubines before sending them away. If he'd literally given "*all that he had*" to Isaac, where could he find anything more to give to the others?

In Genesis 9:3, 4, God informed Noah that "every moving thing that liveth shall be meat [food] for you." Yet we know from other scriptures (Leviticus 11, for example) that "every" in this context was not categorical.

In 1 Timothy 4:4 we find Paul saying that "every creature of God is good, and nothing to be refused, if it be received with thanksgiving," yet none of us would go out and behave as though Paul had given us license to indulge in the indiscriminate consumption of everything we find in the local supermarket, would we?

God commands us through Peter to submit ourselves "to every ordinance of man for the Lord's sake" (1 Peter 2:13). Yet we have a pretty good idea what we're prepared to do when human ordinances conflict with God's, as Peter himself demonstrates for us when he says, "We must obey God rather than men!" (Acts 5:28, 29, NIV; cf. 4:19, 20).

In Romans 14:20 Paul declares that "all food is clean" (NIV). But how does he mean that? If twentieth-century Christians were looking for license to eat whatever they pleased, should they find comfort in this text? Or should they not examine the context of Paul's remarks, and compare scripture with scripture? And when he says in Romans 11:26 that "all Israel will be saved" (NIV), aren't we obligated to make the same kind of evaluation?

In 1 Corinthians 15:27 Paul (citing Psalm 8:6) indicates that God had put "everything" under the feet of Christ. But immediately, he introduces a caveat: "Now when it says that 'everything' had been put under him, it is clear that this does not include God himself" (NIV).

However, when we come to Hebrews 2:17 and similar passages, we seem to take the view that no interpretation is needed. And so steeped are some of us in our cherished position that we have become impenetrable to any theological logic, so to speak, on the matter.

A. T. Jones, as we saw in chapter 2, was forced to confront the implications of insisting on an absolute, 100 percent affinity, and he was forced to do so because of a clear-cut statement by Ellen G. White, to which one questioner had drawn his attention. According to Ellen White: "He [Christ] is a brother in our infirmities, *but not in possessing like passions*" (*Testimonies*, vol. 2, p. 202). If the affinity was absolute, Jones was forced to consider, did it include Jesus' *mind*? Did He have a carnal mind?

We saw how Jones attempted to get around the problem—very unsuccessfully, in my opinion. You cannot insist on 100 percent affinity and then exempt Christ's *mind*. In plain English, that would be complete nonsense. As every schoolchild knows, the mind is *an essential part of the body*. Without it, we have an incomplete person—indeed, a nonperson. If we continue to insist on 100 percent affinity, there is no way to get around this problem. *And we must admit that!*

So we need to recognize that all human speech must be understood within context. When you say to a guest "Make yourself at home—my house and everything in it is yours," you wish to set the visitor at ease and create an atmosphere of informality and relaxation. But you certainly don't mean those words literally. And the sensible guest never takes them as license to go browsing through your drawers or your private papers.

Young friends come to visit, and the parent says to her son, "Take them everywhere! Show them everything! It's your night out on the town! Live it up! Enjoy yourselves!" If a good Adventist parent says this to her responsible Adventist kid, both parties (parent and child) will have a mutual understanding as to what those words connote and what they do not. They'd both know that they do not constitute a license for levity and dissipation. And if the visiting parties are also Christians, they'd understand instinctively that those words of the parent were spoken with clearly understood limits in mind. We'd misunderstand the whole spirit of the message conveyed if we did not know the basic moral and religious convictions of those involved.

With this background in mind, we may understand the phrase "in all things" in Hebrews 2:17 to mean that Christ became like us *in every essential way*. In other words, He was a *real human being*, subject to the vicissitudes, dangers, and limitations that threaten all of us.

The problem with some among us—those for whom Christ's human nature has become an obsession—is that they neglect to consider all the evidence. Their business is so urgent that they have no time to slow down to consider all the facts. *oh, brother!*

In the present discussion, we have not dodged the fact that Jesus was like us. On the contrary, we have presented this evidence—both from the Bible and from the writings of Ellen G. White. On the other hand, however, we dare not sweep under the rug the evidence of Christ's *disaffinity with us*, which we find in Scripture and, as I will now show, in the writings of Ellen G. White as well.

Disaffinity Statements in Ellen G. White

Ellen G. White amazes me again and again. She did not attend any theological school or seminary. She was not trained in systematic theology—and this fact comes through clearly as one reads her voluminous writings. But on the critical aspects of Christian theology, she is straighter and more perceptive than many learned theologians have been throughout the centuries. Here, in a few key statements, is the way she couched the fact of Christ's essential difference from us. In each case, I have emphasized the words most directly pertinent to the point we're developing here.

"He [Christ] was to take His position at the head of humanity by *taking the nature but not the sinfulness of man*" (*The SDA Bible Commentary*, Ellen G. White Comments, vol. 7, p. 925).

"He prayed for His disciples and for Himself, thus identifying Himself with our needs, our weaknesses, and our failings, which are so common with humanity. He was a mighty petitioner, *not possessing the passions of our human, fallen natures*, but compassed with like infirmities, tempted in all points even as we are" (*Testimonies*, vol. 2, pp. 508, 509).

"He is our example in all things. He is a brother in our infirmities, *but not in possessing like passions*. As the sinless One, His nature recoiled from evil" (*ibid.*, p. 202).

Just at this point, before proceeding further, let me interrupt myself to put in juxtaposition Andreasen's contention on this very point, so that you can see for yourself whether all those who claim to have Ellen White on their side really do. Reread the previous two statements from the Spirit of Prophecy and then recall the following statement from Andreasen, quoted in the previous chapter: "*Questions on Doctrine*, p. 383, states that Christ was exempt. The Spirit of Prophecy makes clear that Christ was *not exempt* from the temptations and passions that afflict men. Whoever accepts the new theology must reject the *Testimonies*. There is no choice" (*Letters*, Series A, No. 1, "The Incarnation. Was Christ Exempt?" p. 3).

Can we believe our eyes or not? Is the emperor fully clothed, or is he naked? Here is Ellen White telling us one thing, and Andreasen (who claims to be an authority on her writings) telling us that she taught differently. If I have found this phenomenon once, I have found it a hundred times in the writings of today's Adventist right-wing spokespersons. I am deeply troubled by this irresponsible (one might almost say dishonest) way of handling evidence.

Now, back to the disaffinity statements in Ellen White's writings.

"He took upon Himself human nature, and was tempted in all points as human nature is tempted. He could have sinned; He could have fallen, *but not for one moment was there in Him an evil propensity*" (*The SDA Bible Commentary*, Ellen G. White Comments, vol. 5, p. 1128).[1]

Did She Contradict Herself?

On the face of it, the two sets of affirmations (her affinity and disaffinity statements) seem contradictory. If "evil propensity" (or "passions") refers to an innate or inherent tendency toward sin, a favorable disposition toward it, a leaning or bias in its direction, how can one say that Christ took human nature after 4,000 years of degeneration and yet remained uninfected by this malady, this cancer, this virus that has certainly infected all of us and from which we *all* need deliverance? Did she contradict herself?

A key to the explanation of this apparent contradiction has been suggested by Tim Poirier of the E. G. White Estate (see "Sources Clarify Ellen White's Christology," *Ministry*, December 1989, pp. 7-9). Poirier found in the writings of the Rev. Henry Melvill, one of the authors carefully read by Ellen White as she prepared her material on the Incarnation, a sermon entitled "The Humiliation of the Man Christ Jesus." In this sermon Melvill made the point that the fall had two basic consequences: (1) "innocent infirmities" and (2) "sinful propensities." By "innocent infirmities" Melvill had in mind such characteristics as hunger, pain, weakness, sorrow, and death.[2] Although these are consequence of sin, they are not sinful. For example, sin introduces pain, but pain itself is not sin. These are innocent infirmities. But Melvill also spoke of "sinful propensities." These refer to proneness or tendencies to sin.

In summarizing his position, Melvill made it clear that in his view, Adam had neither innocent infirmities nor sinful propensities. We, on the other hand, were born with both. But Christ took the first (innocent infirmities) but not the second (sinful propensities) (see Poirier, pp. 7, 8).

Therefore, since Ellen G. White was familiar with these distinctions in Melvill's sermon, it seems reasonable to conclude that she used the expression "sinful propensities" in a sense similar to that of Melvill. To delve into the intricacies of formal dictionary definitions, as Larson has done (see *The Word Was Made Flesh*, pp. 23-28), seems labored, forced, and unconvincing.

We may conclude, therefore, that so far as Ellen G. White was concerned, the incarnate Christ was *neither exactly like Adam before the Fall nor exactly like us*. In other words, *He was unique*. This is the simplest and most natural way to understand the apparent contradiction in her statements.

So the final question now is Why—why was Christ unique?

The position of the New Testament is quite clear. The whole world lies "under sin." "There is no one righteous, not even one" (Rom. 3:9, 10, NIV). No one can boast. Every mouth must remain "closed, and all the world become accountable to God" (verse 19, NASB). "By the transgression of the one, death [has] reigned," and "through one man's disobedience the many were made sinners" (Rom. 5:17, 19, NASB). Historically this is what theologians have in mind when they talk about *original sin*.

Admittedly, original sin is not an altogether happy expression. However, some Adventists have denigrated it without careful analysis of its meaning. Fundamentally, the concept of original sin means that on account of Adam's fall the entire human race has been *infected* by sin and that therefore the entire world (including infants) stands in need of a Saviour. ⌐from Birth⌐

Without using the expression "original sin" (and perhaps fortunately so), Ellen G. White refers, nevertheless, to the same human predicament described by the apostle and by theologians for centuries: "By inheritance and example the sons become partakers of the father's sin. Wrong tendencies, perverted appetites, and debased morals . . . are transmitted as a legacy from father to son, to the third and fourth generation" (*Patriarchs and Prophets*, p. 306). "While they [Adam and Eve] were obedient to God, the evil one could not harm them. . . . But should they once yield to temptation, their nature would become . . . depraved" (*ibid.*, p. 53).

She describes sin as "leprosy, . . . deep-rooted, deadly, and impossible to be cleansed by human power." Everyone has been infected, she says. "But Jesus, coming to dwell in humanity, *receives no pollution*. His presence has healing virtue for the sinner" (*The Desire of Ages*, p. 266; italics supplied).

As we saw from the first set of statements that we cited from Ellen G. White, she vigorously defended the fact of Christ's affinity with us, His identification with us in our human predicament. In my classes in Christology, I never tired of placing emphasis on one particular statement of hers, whose nineteenth-century literary quaintness makes it even stronger in its emphasis: "Christ *did not make-believe take human nature*," she said. "He did verily take it—He did in reality possess human nature" (*The SDA Bible Commentary*, Ellen G. White Comments, vol. 5, p. 1130; italics supplied).

But like a parent who, after emphasizing to her children departing for college the need to buckle down and study hard, balances her strong counsel with the importance of recreation and diversion, Ellen G. White found it necessary to bring us back to center with a series of carefully crafted cautions, as we have now seen.

Her most telling statement regarding the uniqueness of Christ—and one that some authors have struggled hard to stifle or explain away with far-fetched explanations[3]—came in an 1895 letter to Pastor and Mrs. W.L.H. Baker, American missionaries then serving in Tasmania.

Speaking about the transmission of sin, she wrote: "These dear children received from Adam an inheritance of disobedience, of guilt and death." Did Christ share the same experience? Her response was strong and emphatic: "Be careful, exceedingly careful as to how you dwell on the human nature of Christ. Do not set Him before the people as a man with the propensities of sin. He is the second Adam. The first Adam was created a pure, sinless being, without a taint of sin upon him; he was in the image of God. He could fall, and he did fall through transgressing. *Because of sin, his posterity was born with inherent propensities of disobedience.* But Jesus Christ was the only begotten Son of God. He took upon Himself human nature, and was tempted in all points as human nature is tempted. He could have sinned; He could have fallen, but not for one moment was there in Him an evil propensity" (*The SDA Bible Commentary*, Ellen G. White Comments, vol. 5, p. 1128; italics supplied; see also *Ellen G. White Manuscript Releases*, vol. 13, pp. 14-30).

Clearly meaning to explain how it was possible for Christ to bypass this universal infection of sin, she continued by emphasizing that the birth of Jesus was completely different from ours—"a miracle of God," she said, citing Luke 1:31-35. That passage in Luke ends with these words from Gabriel's lips: "The Holy Spirit will come upon you, and the power of the Most High will overshadow you; and for that reason the holy offspring shall be called the Son of God" (Luke 1:35, NASB).

"These words," she said, "do not refer to any human being, except to the Son of the infinite God" (*ibid.*).[4]

Then follows her strongest warning in the letter: *"It is a mystery that is left unexplained to mortals that Christ* could be tempted in all points like as we are, and yet be without sin. *The incarnation of Christ has ever been, and will ever remain, a mystery.* That which is revealed is for us and for our children, *but let every human being be warned from the ground of making Christ altogether human, such an one as ourselves; for it cannot be"* (*ibid.*, pp. 1128, 1129; italics supplied).

And the reason for this uniqueness is simple. He came not merely to set us an *example*, but to be our *Saviour*. If He were altogether like us—100 percent—if He had shared in exactly the same way the inheritance of sin and guilt we all received from Adam, then He would have been crippled as a Saviour. But more than that, He would Himself have stood in need of a Redeemer. But, says Ellen White, "He needed no atonement" (*Review and Herald*, Sept. 21, 1886; see also *Questions on Doctrine*, p. 677).

He was "holy, blameless, pure, set apart from sinners," not needing, like the ancient priests, "to offer sacrifices . . . for his own sins." The ancient economy appointed priests who needed to contend with their own weakness. But God appointed Jesus, "who has been made perfect forever" (Heb. 7:26-28, NIV).

So Jesus came as a real human being. *A human being in every essential sense of the word.* One *with* us, but not one *of* us. "In all things like unto us, sin only [experiential *and* inherited] excepted"—to be for us a Saviour and an Example.

And what really did we need more? Was it an example? Or was it a Saviour? For me, it was a Saviour. I thank God with my whole heart for sending Him as my Example. But I thank God even more for sending Him as my Saviour!

---

[1] Ralph Larson has gone to great lengths in an effort to deflect the impact of these propensity statements. See *The Word Was Made Flesh*, pages 23-28. I find his explanations artificial and contrived.

[2] Melvill's reference here to hunger, pain, sorrow, and death should probably be understood against the background of Revelation 21:4. Here, speaking about the final restoration, the prophet says that "there shall be no more death, neither sorrow, nor crying, neither shall there be any more pain: for the former things are passed away." To conclude from Melvill's statement that he believed the unfallen Adam to be devoid of pain receptors, for instance, or that he was beyond the sensation of hunger, would be unwarranted. At any rate, the correctness of Melvill's theology is not the issue here. Our aim, rather, is to determine the meaning of Ellen White's "propensity" statements.

[3] See *The Word Was Made Flesh*, pp. 324-328, where Larson suggests that Baker's problem was adoptionism, a third-century heresy which suggested that Christ was not the Son of God at birth, but rather was subsequently *adopted* by the Father and Son. The evidence given by Larson for this far-fetched explanation is ingenious but totally fabricated.

[4] By contrast, Ron Spear, for example, holds that "Christ received from His mother, Mary, the same fallen human nature that we receive from our mothers" (*Our Firm Foundation*, August 1993, p. 2).

Chapter 5

THE TEMPTATIONS OF CHRIST:
Did He Have an Advantage
Over Us?

How should we understand the temptations of Christ in view of our conclusion that He did not have any inherited passions or propensities to sin, as all of us have? Was it possible for Him to sin? And if not, how could His temptations be real? Without sinful passions or propensities, did He have an advantage that we don't have insofar as the power of temptation is concerned? And if so, then how could the book of Hebrews present His temptations as a major factor in His qualification as our High Priest? (See Heb. 2:17, 18; 5:7-9; 4:15.) How did Christ overcome temptation, anyway? And how does that relate to us and the temptations we face today? These questions form the backdrop of what I intend to cover in this chapter.

Was it possible for Christ to sin? This is the most fundamental of all the questions just raised.

Surprising as it may appear to some, the Bible supplies no explicit answer to this specific question. It merely presents the fact that Christ was severely tempted. I suppose, however, that if you were to ask the biblical writers, they would respond with a measure of surprise. "Why do you ask?" they'd say. "Haven't we already answered that question? If we say that He was tempted, what else can we mean?"

For some reason, however, Christians throughout the centuries have evidenced much confusion on this issue.

E. J. Waggoner, of 1888 fame, had trouble with the concept, claiming that Christ could not sin (see *Signs of the Times*, Jan. 21, 1889, p. 39). And the eminent Reformed systematic theologian Louis Berkhof maintained that although Christ's temptations were real, it was not possible for Him to sin. Wrote Berkhof: "We may not detract [meaning, we should not detract] from the reality of the temptations of Jesus as the last Adam, however difficult it may be to conceive of one who could not sin being tempted" (*Systematic Theology*, p. 338).

Like Berkhof, Ellen G. White took the position that the temptations of Christ were real. But unlike this learned theologian (and unlike E. J. Waggoner), she affirmed that it *was possible* for Him to yield. "The temptations to which Christ was subjected," she said, "were a terrible reality. As a free agent, He was placed on probation, with liberty to yield to Satan's temptations and to work at cross purposes with God. If this were not so, if it had not been possible for Him to fall, He could not have been tempted in all points as the human family is tempted" (*The SDA Bible Commentary*, Ellen G. White Comments, vol. 5, p. 1082).

And she was not unaware of the enormous implications of this reality. Notice this extraordinary statement: "Satan in heaven had hated Christ for His position in the courts of God. He hated Him the more when he himself was dethroned. He hated Him who pledged Himself to redeem a race of sinners. Yet into the world where Satan claimed dominion God permitted His Son to come, a helpless babe, subject to the weakness of humanity. He permitted Him to meet life's peril in common with every human soul, to fight the battle as every child of humanity must fight it, *at the risk of failure and eternal loss*" (*The Desire of Ages*, p. 49; italics supplied).

This is a difficult concept for some to accept, as I discovered after preaching my very first sermon as a young ministerial intern, in which I made reference to that last statement. One brother accosted me following the service, and for about 10 minutes lambasted me for taking that position. "Mrs. White did not know what she was talking about," he said. "It was impossible for Christ to sin." But the Bible makes it clear that the temptations of Christ were absolutely real and that Satan dogged Jesus' steps throughout His earthly life.

Nature and Purpose of Christ's Temptations

According to Scripture, Christ was "in all points tempted like as we are, yet without sin" (Heb. 4:15).

What does this mean?

"The translation in the King James Version really does not do justice to the Greek," an Adventist New Testament scholar said to me recently. "*Kata panta*, the expression used in the passage, is extremely difficult to convert to English."

"But we have to translate it," I pressed him.

"Well, that's why we have people study Greek—so that they don't have to translate it. But the best we've been able to come up with is that Jesus was tempted *'variously and intensively,'* an expression that (given the person Christ was) emphasizes the rigor and intensity of the temptations He had to endure." *

That makes sense to me, but I suspect that such a radical departure from the usual translation might be too much for many readers. So allow me to deal with the issue on the basis of the familiar translation in the King James Version: He "was in all points tempted like as we are."

Does this mean that Christ experienced every single specific temptation that I face? I don't think so. There are factors that render a specific temptation different—not unique, but different.

For example, temptations are sometimes related to *time*. The temptation to hold slaves or to be a pirate is not generally as strong today as it once was. And I rather doubt that Jesus was bothered by either.

Then there is the question of *place*. The specific temptations that confront a person living in metropolitan Manila, London, or New York today could hardly be the same as those that faced Christ in the small, rural village of Nazareth in the first century. Not that Nazareth was a paradise, of course. Remember that some wondered whether any good thing could come from there (John 1:46). But the anonymity afforded by the huge metropolises of today was completely unknown in Christ's time.

Then, third, there is the question of *personality and life setting*. Christ could not have had the particular temptations of a woman, for example. He never had to face the issue of aborting a fetus. Christ was never a human father, had never been married, and, therefore, did not meet the particular temptations of a father—with teenagers, say. Or of a husband or wife having to live with a difficult or impossible spouse.

When the Scriptures speak of Christ as having been "in all points tempted like as we are," we are not to think of a *multitude* of "points." Rather, we are to think of just *three major points*, summarized neatly, I think, in 1 John 2:15, 16: "Do not love the world, nor the things in the world. If anyone loves the world, the love of the Father is not in him. For all that is in the world, the lust of the flesh and the lust of the eyes and the boastful pride of life, is not from the Father, but is from the world" (NASB).

The lust (*epithumia*) of the flesh has to do with the desire, the drive, the longing, of humanity's sensual nature. It refers to the craving of the flesh for the indulgence of evil and sin (see *The SDA Bible Commentary*, vol. 7, p. 642).

The lust (*epithumia*) of the eyes may be a reference to mental pleasure stimulated through sight. A great deal of sinful pleasure today is experienced through the eyes. Evidently it has always been that way. Many who will not participate in open sin, for one reason or the other, nevertheless enjoy reading about it, studying it in pictures, or watching it depicted on the movie screen (*ibid.*).

The pride (*alazoneia*) of life refers to the vainglory, the ostentation, the display of worldly goods and materialistic trappings—the preoccupation with the creature comforts of life. It suggests the substitution of the material and transitory for the spiritual and eternal (*ibid.*).

These are the three major areas in which we are tempted. There is no temptation that faces us which does not fall within one or more of these three categories. And when the Bible says that Jesus was tempted in all points like as we are, it means to say that He was buffeted in these three major areas. And we can see this in the three primary temptations that He encountered in the wilderness at the commencement of His ministry.

The Three Categories of Temptation

The *first* temptation He faced in the wilderness had to do with the lust of the flesh.

The setting is familiar. Jesus had just been baptized. The Holy

Spirit (in the form of a dove) appeared from heaven, acknowledging Him as the Son of God. He retired to the wilderness for meditation and contemplation upon His mission. How would He proceed with His ministry? Would He employ the means that the Jews were expecting? Or would He follow His Father's plan for Him? These were some of the issues that weighed upon His mind as He went out into the wasteland of Judea.

Matthew 4:1 says that "Jesus was led by the Spirit into the desert *to be tempted by the devil*" (NIV). *It was God's purpose* that Jesus should undergo this special period of temptation and testing now — at the beginning of His ministry. In the words of R.C.H. Lenski: "The devil was to exert the full extent of his power, God offering no restraint." "Like Job, Jesus was placed into Satan's power so that the latter might tempt Him to the uttermost" (*The Interpretation of St. Matthew's Gospel*, pp. 139, 148).

"If you are the Son of God," said the devil to Jesus after He'd been fasting for 40 days, "tell these stones to become bread" (Matt. 4:3, NIV). Though the fundamental issue here lay beneath the surface, as we will see, the immediate appeal was to the flesh — to its lust, its craving. And every temptation that accosts us in the area of the physical or sensual appetite falls under this first category.

However, while appetite was clearly the occasion or context of Jesus' first temptation, the issue went much deeper — to that of *autonomy and independence* from God. That was the real test, of which appetite was only the springboard. In John 6:57, Christ said: "I live because of the Father" (NIV). He "was surrendered to the Father's will, and dependent upon His power." "Utterly . . . emptied of self . . . He made no plans for Himself," but "accepted God's plan for Him" as the Father unfolded it day by day (Ellen G. White, *The Desire of Ages*, p. 208).

Satan's strategy in this first temptation, then — as indeed in the two that followed — was to shake this utter dependence and to lead the Saviour to take matters into His own hands, enticing Him to demonstrate His divine power outside and independent of God. As Ellen White put it, Satan's purpose was to "shake the confidence of Christ in His Father. . . . Satan hoped to insinuate doubt as to His

Father's love" (*Selected Messages*, book 1, p. 275).

But Christ turned away from this subtle scheme. "It is written," He said, "'Man does not live on bread alone'" (Luke 4:4, NIV).

The second temptation centered on the *pride of life*, the third element in John's trio of pitfalls.

Here the devil transported Christ to the pinnacle of the Temple and dared Him to demonstrate His Messiahship by hurling Himself down headlong, counting on God's protection (Matt. 4:5, 6).

From a psychological standpoint, the move was perfectly logical, and we see here the same cunning demonstrated in the Garden of Eden. It was as if the devil was saying to Christ: "You are claiming complete dependence upon the Father. Now prove it! The time has come for You to show Your faith. Show it!" It was an appeal to human pride and vainglory.

But again, the basic question was that of *dependence and surrender* versus *independence and autonomy*. Jesus maintained His ground, refusing to do anything unbidden by the Father.

The third temptation involved both the lust of the eyes and the pride of life.

Here the devil took Jesus to "a very high mountain and showed him all the kingdoms of the world and their splendor," and he said to Him, "All this I will give you . . . if you will bow down and worship me" (Matt. 4:8, 9, NIV).

This was a temptation to govern the world without dying on the cross. It was a temptation to do what He had come to do, but in a way that was contrary to God's plan (see *Selected Messages*, book 1, pp. 286, 287). This was the kind of kingdom that the Jews were expecting at the time, and it would have been "politically correct" for Jesus to succumb to such an overture. The dazzle and splendor of worldly kingdoms passed before His eyes, a stark contrast to His present dismal state. It was an appeal to human pride and to our craving for luxury, for ease, for the creature comforts of life.

The subtle suggestion in all three temptations, then, was that Jesus should depart from God's plan and take matters into His own hands. Indeed, the temptation to autonomy and independence from God is the essence of sin, and it lies at the root of the entire tragedy of evil.

The three temptations in the wilderness—which fall so neatly into John's three categories—were only the first round in what was to be a constant hounding of Jesus by the forces of hell. Thus in recording the end of this first series of temptations, Luke says that the devil left Christ "for a season" (Luke 4:13). Or, as it appears in the *New American Standard Bible*, "until an opportune time." This clearly shows that the wilderness encounter was not to be the devil's only onslaught on the Saviour. And, indeed, the Bible does record other instances of fierce combat between Jesus and the underworld.

Some of the cases are subtle and well-nigh unrecognizable but for a few illuminating insights that we find in the writings of Ellen G. White.

Temptations to Alter or Abort His Mission

Matthew informs us that on the road to Caesarea Philippi Jesus intimated to His disciples the manner of His impending death. Reacting strongly to the announcement, "Peter took Him aside and began to rebuke Him, saying, 'God forbid it, Lord! This shall never happen to You'"(Matt. 16:21-23, NASB).

In His response, surprisingly, Jesus addressed Himself to "Satan" and not "Peter." "Get behind Me, Satan!" (verse 23, NASB). Commenting on this apparently unremarkable incident, Ellen White offers this illuminating comment: "Satan was trying to discourage Jesus, and turn Him from His mission; and Peter, in his blind love, was giving voice to the temptation. The prince of evil was the author of the thought. His instigation was behind that impulsive appeal. In the wilderness, Satan had offered Christ the dominion of the world on condition of forsaking the path of humiliation and sacrifice. . . . And through Peter, Satan was again pressing the temptation upon Jesus. . . . Satan had [actually] interposed between Peter and his Master" (*The Desire of Ages*, p. 416).

Luke 9:51 describes another major temptation encounter not usually recognized as such. The text says simply that "it came about, when the days were approaching for His ascension, that He resolutely set His face to go to Jerusalem" (NASB).

The clue that something important is taking place lies in the clause "He resolutely set His face." The words imply a struggle. They suggest that Christ was facing something for which He needed to brace Himself. Commenting on this situation, Ellen White gives the following insight into Luke's apparently matter-of-fact observation. I quote her at length.

"To the heart of Christ it was a bitter task to press His way against the fears, disappointment, and unbelief of His beloved disciples. It was hard to lead them forward to the anguish and despair that awaited them at Jerusalem. *And Satan was at hand to press his temptations upon the Son of man.* Why should He now go to Jerusalem, to certain death? All around Him were souls hungering for the bread of life. On every hand were suffering ones waiting for His word of healing. The work to be wrought by the gospel of His grace was but just begun. And He was full of the vigor of manhood's prime. Why not go forward to the vast fields of the world with the words of His grace, the touch of His healing power? . . . Why leave the harvest gathering to His disciples, so weak in faith, so dull of understanding, so slow to act? Why face death now, and leave the work in its infancy? *The foe who in the wilderness had confronted Christ assailed Him now with fierce and subtle temptations. Had Jesus yielded for a moment, had He changed His course in the least particular to save Himself, Satan's agencies would have triumphed, and the world would have been lost"* (*ibid.*, p. 486; italics supplied).

Another intense moment of special temptation occurred in connection with the request of certain Greek visitors to Jerusalem (John 12:20-23). The circumstances surrounding their visit are not explained, and most readers would pass over the report of their inquiry without much thought. But beneath the surface were struggles as fierce as a raging tempest. And the following remarks again bring this out: "The message of the Greeks, foreshadowing as it did the gathering of the Gentiles, brought to the mind of Jesus His entire mission. The work of redemption passed before Him, from the time when in heaven the plan was laid, to the death that was now so near at hand. *A mysterious cloud seemed to enshroud the Son of God. Its gloom was felt by those near Him. He sat rapt in thought. At last the silence was broken by His mournful voice, 'Now is my soul troubled; and what shall I say? Father, save me from this hour.'* In anticipation Christ was already *drinking the cup of bitterness. His humanity shrank from the hour of aban-donment, when to all appearance He would be deserted even by God*" (*ibid.*, p. 624; italics supplied).

The struggle in the Garden of Gethsemane represented the final, titanic showdown of Christ's earthly ministry. Recognizing that the game was almost over, the devil pulled out all the stops. That night, the entire attention of the hosts of hell was focused on one place and one place only—the Garden of Gethsemane. Athens was free of devils that evening, I think. And so also were Rome and Corinth and Ephesus and all the cities, towns, and hamlets of the world. I see the following words from Ellen White as applicable to that night, in particular: "The serpent himself made Christ the mark of every weapon of hell" (*The SDA Bible Commentary*, Ellen G. White Comments, vol. 5, p. 1080).

"And being in agony," Luke wrote of Christ in that critical hour, "He was praying very fervently; and His sweat became like drops of blood, falling down upon the ground" (Luke 22:44, NASB). "Let this cup pass from Me," He prayed again and again (Matt. 26:39, 42, 44, NASB).

"*Terrible was the temptation* to let the human race bear the conse-quences of its own guilt, while He stood innocent before God" (*The Desire of Ages*, p. 688; italics supplied). "The humanity of the Son of God trembled in that trying hour. He prayed not now for His disci-ples that their faith might not fail, *but for His own tempted, agonized soul.* The awful moment had come—that moment which was to de-cide the destiny of the world. The fate of humanity trembled in the balance. *Christ might even now refuse to drink the cup* apportioned to guilty man. It was not yet too late" (*ibid.*, p. 690; italics supplied).

But Christ came through victorious. "If this cannot pass away unless I drink it, Thy will be done," He said (Matt. 26:42, NASB). And "having made the decision," Ellen White writes, "He fell dying to the ground" (*ibid.*, p. 693). And He'd have died right there be-neath the olive trees outside Jerusalem, crushed by the weight of the sin of the world—something we can express, but cannot under-stand—had not an angel come to strengthen Him (Luke 22:43).

I've gone into the foregoing detail vis à vis the temptations of

Jesus so as to make this one point: *For any of us to think, even for a moment, that the temptations we face can be compared, in intensity, to those that Christ endured is patently ludicrous.*

Was It a Charade?

Some among us feel that unless Christ was altogether — 100 percent — like us, then His temptations were nothing but a sham, a charade. This conclusion is completely misguided. One does not have to be sinful in order to be tempted. One need not have sinful passions or propensities in order to be tempted. The only prerequisite for genuine temptation to occur is that the subject have the capacity to sin. And, as we have shown, the clear implication of Scripture and the explicit position of Ellen White is that Jesus had such a capacity. Why else would Satan have struggled so hard and so persistently with Him? God is not into playacting. He does not engage in sham. If Christ could not sin, then the whole purpose of His coming would have been compromised.

But someone might say, We grant that He could have sinned. That is not our argument. Our contention, rather, is that without sinful passions and propensities, He would have had an advantage that the rest of us don't have!

I must confess to becoming just a little bit flustered whenever I hear talk about "advantage." As though salvation were some contest in which we're running competition with Christ. *He came to be our Saviour.* So what if it turned out that He had an advantage? Who but the devil should care about that?

But did He really "have an advantage"? The answer is no!

For example, although the temptations we face fall into the identical three categories that He had to meet, the fact that He was the God-man exposed Him to special, specific temptations unknown to us. I have never been tempted, for instance, to use my divine power to extricate myself from difficulty, because I have none. But Christ had to meet that temptation daily, and He felt it keenly.

Commenting on this point, Ellen White had this to say: "He had received honor in the heavenly courts, and was familiar with absolute power. It was as difficult for Him to keep the level of humanity as for men to rise above the low level of their depraved natures, and be partakers of the divine nature. Christ," she said, "was to be put to the closest test, requiring the strength of all His faculties to resist the inclination when in danger, to use His power to deliver Himself from peril, and triumph over the power of the prince of darkness" (*The SDA Bible Commentary*, Ellen G. White Comments, vol. 7, p. 930).

For another thing, we are tainted with sin, but He was not. This was *not* an advantage for Him, as many thoughtlessly conclude today. That He was untainted with sin made His reaction to sin much more sensitive than ours. When we buy a brand-new car, we are very particular for the first few weeks or months about where we park it. Usually, we keep it well away from other vehicles, to protect it from dents or scratches. It is a nerve-racking time for the new owner—until the first scratch or dent. By the second or third scrape, we find our nervousness subsiding, and the common laxity of the regular car owner sets in.

It was with the tension of a person with a brand-new car, so to speak, that Christ had to live every second of His earthly life. The faintest "scratch," the slightest "dent," would scuttle His entire mission. How would you like to go through life with the consciousness that a single misstep on your part would imperil the salvation of the whole human race? But that, precisely, was Christ's daily lot.

Only the building that withstands the earthquake or the storm knows the full intensity of the invading force. And only the person who resists and withstands temptation on any point knows its full strength and power.

In the diagrams that follow, Diagram A represents the experience of all of us. If 10 stands for the full strength of a particular temptation, most of us in too many areas of our lives succumb before the pressure rises to the degree of, say, 6. But in the case of Christ (Diagram B), the pressure rose to the tenth degree on each and every temptation—for He never yielded once.

"Christ was tempted by Satan in a hundredfold severer manner than was Adam, and under circumstances in every way more trying" (*My Life Today*, p. 323). "While He was free from the taint of

Temptation's Richter Scale

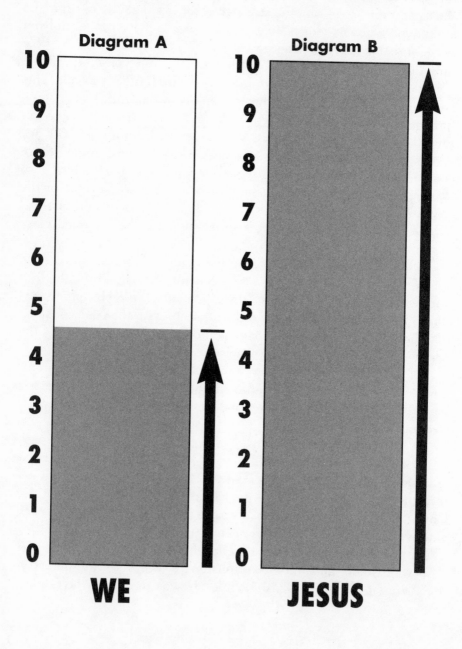

Diagram A

Diagram B

WE

JESUS

sin," Ellen White said, "the refined sensibilities of His holy nature rendered contact with evil *unspeakably painful to Him*" (Ellen G. White, *Review and Herald*, Nov. 8, 1887; italics supplied). No, He did *not* "have an advantage over us"!

So how does all this relate to the issues mentioned at the beginning of the chapter?

I think the following points have now become clear: Christ *did* have the capacity to sin. Thus His temptations were real. He did *not* have an advantage over us, in so far as the power of temptation is concerned. On the contrary, the temptations He bore were much stronger and more intense. And, of course, infinitely more critical. But He overcame temptation in the same way that is open to all of us—through God's inexhaustible power, which the Holy Spirit makes available.

And yet we must ever keep in mind that *His victory is our victory*. That is to say, *we are saved by His victory*. We are saved as we participate *in* His victory—as we, in other words, accept His victory as our own. We are not saved by trying to duplicate His victory. Instead, *we are saved by accepting His victory as our own*. We cannot emphasize this too strongly.

"He saved us, not on the basis of deeds which we have done in righteousness, but according to His mercy, by the washing of regeneration and renewing by the Holy Spirit, whom He poured out upon us richly through Jesus Christ our Savior, that being justified by His grace we might be made heirs according to the hope of eternal life" (Titus 3:5-7, NASB).

We seek personal victory *not in order to be saved*, but because of an insatiable desire, born of profound gratitude, *to be like Him who has saved us*. And we know that by beholding we can become changed into His image, "from glory to glory even as by the Spirit of the Lord" (2 Cor. 3:18).

---

* Summarized from a personal conversation with Dr. Warren Trenchard of Canadian Union College, October 1993.

Chapter 6

WHAT IS SIN?:
The Issue at the Heart
of the Debate

I f you were to ask the typical Adventist for a definition of sin, the immediate response would be: "Sin is the transgression of the law." This answer, taken verbatim from 1 John 3:4, is correct, of course.

The problem, however, is that a certain group of Adventists operate as though this definition comprehended all that could be said about sin. According to one of them, "the only way we can identify sin is by the law. Our prophet Ellen White says there is but one definition and that is found in 1 John 3:4" (Ron Spear, "The New Theology: A False Gospel," *Our Firm Foundation*, March 1993, p. 12). So, based on this one definition alone, some of our brethren have come to understand sin primarily in terms of *behavior*, in terms of *acts* that we commit.

Other Adventists, however, while accepting the Johannine definition of sin just given, also see the phenomenon as something deeper, more comprehensive than that simple definition would lead us to conclude. And it seems to me that the tension between these two understandings of sin (the narrow and the broad—not to say the shallow and the deep) lies at the heart of the perennial debate over sanctification, perfection, and Christ's nature in the Adventist Church. From the restricted definition of sin come admonitions to "stop sinning" that have become a characteristic staple among a certain group of Adventists.

Defrocked Adventist evangelist Albion Fox Ballenger (1861-1921) was among them. His favorite theme during his heyday was the coming of the Spirit. Frustrated over what he saw as a lack of power in the church, he thought he had put his finger on the cause. "We cannot have apostolic power in the church until we have apostolic purity," he said. All the Achans, Judases, and Ananiases must be eliminated. "First a holy church, [then] the Holy Ghost" (*Signs of the Times*, Nov. 15, 1899, p. 738). In a speech to a General Conference session in 1899, Ballenger was even more explicit: "Righteousness by faith was given us of God *to stop our sinning*. Let no man say he has received righteousness by faith until he has stopped sinning" ("Victory," *General Conference Bulletin*, 1899, p. 96; emphasis Ballenger's).

In this emphasis, M. L. Andreasen followed in Ballenger's footsteps. Andreasen saw baptism as the sixth "step" to Christ, the step in which the sinner is fully "cleansed, purified, justified," and made dead to sin. From that point, the new convert is to "abstain from sin" (*A Faith to Live By*, pp. 96-99; cf. *The Faith of Jesus*, pp. 69-97). In one place, he boldly admonished converts to "get rid of every sin," to "gain the victory over every besetment," to "break every chain that binds," and to "do it *now*, today" (*The Gospel Prophet*, Vol. II, p. 78).

This is precisely the kind of emphasis we find in the so-called right-wing movement within Adventism today.

"Our High Priest," wrote Wieland and Short, "cannot forever minister His blood in substitution to cover the perpetual sinning of His people" (*1888 Re-examined*, p. 156). What these two gentlemen mean to imply here is that sinning must stop. "1 John 2:1 says that for His people to stop sinning is the purpose of His sacrifice on the cross" (*ibid.*, p. 195). God's people must overcome as Christ overcame, argued Wieland. "They must have ceased to continue sinning" (*The 1888 Message*, p. 94).

In the words of Colin and Russell Standish, "a central theme of the new *Adventism* is that we will continue to sin until the Second Coming" (*Adventism Vindicated*, p. 63). But not so, say the brothers. "Christ demonstrated beyond all dispute that sinlessness in this life is no chimera when a man is under the power of the indwelling Spirit" (*ibid.*, p. 65).

And issue after issue of *Our Firm Foundation* carries forward this theme. Some "preachers tell us," says Ron Spear, that "we will be sinning and confessing without overcoming until Jesus comes." This is "the New Theology," he reasons. But according to the plan of redemption, the Holy Spirit gives power to keep the repentant soul "from sinning" (*Our Firm Foundation*, March 1993, pp. 12, 13).

Not So Simple

Adventists should have no problem with 1 John 3:4. Sin is, indeed, the transgression of the law. But neither should we have difficulty with the more complex definitions of sin that we find in the rest of Scripture.

In Romans, for example, we read that "everything that does not come from faith is sin" (Rom. 14:23, NIV). Here we're no longer in the legal, forensic realm, as in 1 John 3:4. Rather, we have moved to the *relational* realm, the area of trust, of faith. "What would have happened to Adventism," asks Richard Coffen, "had our pioneers latched onto Paul's definition of sin here instead of John's? Would we have been so easily influenced by legalism?" (Richard W. Coffen in a personal letter to me, Aug. 18, 1993).

For me, one of the most instructive passages in this connection is found in Psalm 32, one of David's great penitential prayers. Overwhelmed by his need of God's forgiving grace, David passionately bared his soul before his great Redeemer. And the vocabulary he employed, under the Spirit, has helped enrich our understanding of the complex ramifications of this universal human predicament we know as sin.

Says David: "Blessed is he whose *transgression* is forgiven, whose *sin* is covered. Blessed is the man unto whom the Lord imputeth not *iniquity*, and in whose spirit there is no *guile*" (Ps. 32:1, 2). The four terms highlighted in this scripture bring to our attention four separate nuances of the sin problem. Here's a brief description.

1. *Transgression* (Hebrew *pesha'*) signifies "'rebellion,' departure from God," and hence implies "willful sin" (*The SDA Bible Commentary*, vol. 2, p. 706). "By all counts," says the *Interpreter's Dictionary of the Bible*, "*pesha'* is the Old Testament's most profound word for 'sin,' indicating its theological meaning as 'revolt against God'" (vol. R-Z, p. 362). It is not "a mere failure or mistake like . . .

[*chatta'ah*], since it consists of wilful disobedience" (*ibid.*).

2. *Sin* (Hebrew *chatta'ah*, equivalent to *hamartia* in the New Testament) refers to "sin from the point of view of missing the mark, failing to do one's duty" (*The SDA Bible Commentary*, vol. 3, p. 706; cf. *Interpreter's Dictionary of the Bible*, vol. R-Z, p. 361).

3. *Iniquity* (Hebrew *'awon*) refers to "'moral distortion,' 'crookedness,' 'guilt'" (*The SDA Bible Commentary*, vol. 3, p. 707). It speaks of an *inner* state that is deformed, perverse, twisted (see *Interpreter's Dictionary of the Bible*, vol. R-Z, p. 362).

4. *Guile* (Hebrew *remiyyah*) means deceit, falsehood, duplicity.

This list is far from exhaustive. After discussing at least 12 different terms for sin in the Old Testament, the *Interpreter's Dictionary of the Bible* notes that even that did "not at all exhaust the vocabulary of sin in the O[ld] T[estament]" (*ibid.*). And often, observes the same source, the "various words for 'sin' are . . . heaped together as synonyms," thereby losing, especially "when employed in poetic parallelism," "the sharp edge of their distinctive meanings" (*ibid.*).

Nevertheless, the four terms used by David provide us with conceptual windows into the *principal dimensions* of the reality we know as sin. The forms are not simply synonymous, as would usually be the case in Hebrew poetry. Rather, they spell out for us the multifaceted parameters of this universal malady, and they show that the matter is deeper and far more chronic and complex than some have understood it.

Once one understands this, one does not issue—as did Andreasen—facile admonitions to "get rid of every sin" and "do it now, today"! Such simplistic pietism, well-meaning though it may be, is irresponsible and can actually have the unintended result of seriously discouraging those who are struggling with powerful inherited and cultivated tendencies to evil.

If we are talking about sin as *pesha'* (departure from God, rebellion, defiance, willful transgression), then it is quite obvious that true Christians should have put such practices and attitudes behind them. While this does not mean that we will never know times of relapse into *pesha'*, it does mean to say that the true follower of the Lord has set a course that runs in the direction of God's will. The spirit of defiance—of stubborn resistance and rebellion—has surrendered. And the mature Christian can now say with the hymn writer Mrs. C. H. Morris:

"My stubborn will at last has yielded,
   I would be thine, and thine alone.
   And this the prayer my lips are bringing:
   'Lord, let in me Thy will be done.'

"Sweet will of God, still fold me closer,
   Till I am wholly lost in Thee."

Those who come to the place where these words truly reflect the sentiments of the heart are on the way to heaven. With them, all transgressions, all revolt against God, all willful defiance of His rule have ceased. With them, rebellion will not arise the second time. They are, as some say, *safe to save*.

But are they, necessarily, "perfect" or "sinless" here and now? No, because there are other dimensions of sin to reckon with. There is *chatta'ah*, for example, falling short, failing to do one's duty, missing the mark. And as a colleague of mine has remarked, "Missing the mark need not necessarily be restricted to 'falling short,' but can also refer to going beyond." "As in archery," he said, "I may miss the mark when my arrow fails to reach the target, goes beyond the target, or goes to either side of the target." If we take this metaphor seriously, he observed, "then sin not only can refer to falling short of the goal (laxness or liberalism, perhaps?) but also it can refer to going beyond what is required (legalism or conservatism, perhaps?)." "Punctiliousness," he concludes, "may be as much a moral blemish as permissiveness" (Coffen, a personal letter to me, Aug. 18, 1993).

Are We Perfect When We Do Nothing Bad?
There might be days when we may not be able to point to anything bad that we have done. But if we're honest, we'd sense that we're not free from what we usually call "sins of omission."

What are these sins of omission? Dr. W.G.C. Murdoch used to

tell about the little boy who, when asked this question, replied: "Sins of omission are sins I should have committed, but didn't." You can be sure that little boy is not the only one confused about this intangible reality!

Sins of omission refer to the positive duties we neglect to do: the wrong we might have checked, but failed to; the good we might have done, but didn't; the downward trend in some person's life that we might have stopped by some kind word or deed left unspoken or undone.

Who of us, at the end of the day, can truthfully say: "I've done *all* that God expected of me today. I've not missed the mark in a single instance"? And with thousands dying daily for want of food, shelter, or clothing—while some of us have plenty, who among us can truthfully say at the close of the day, "Father, I've today used my means and influence to full capacity in bringing relief and succor to the suffering"?

I recently read a news item that struck me as significant. It was reporting on the publication of the annual list of Britain's richest people. As in the past, the report said, Queen Elizabeth headed the list, with something like $8 billion. Since the queen is a public figure, I will take the liberty of using her situation to illustrate what I'm talking about here.

In my estimation, the queen of England is one of the most decent people in the world. You won't find her engaged in gossip or brawls; you won't find her in nightclubs or pubs. As for carousing and wild parties, don't even mention them. Foul language never crosses her lips, and she is abusive to no one. The epitome of purity and high morals, she commands the respect of the whole world, notwithstanding the foibles and failings of members of the royal family in recent years.

But with millions starving to death today, think of the queen approaching Jesus (with $8 billion stashed away in various banks and securities) and asking Him: "Good Master, what must I do to have eternal life?" What do you think Jesus would say to Her Majesty?

I'm not passing judgment, so please don't misunderstand me. But in a similar encounter while here on earth, Jesus asked as follows: "If you want to enter life, obey the commandments" (Matt. 19:17, NIV).

"Which ones?" the wealthy young man answered, confident of his impeccable record. "All these I have kept," he said (after Jesus had given him the list he sought). "What do I still lack?"

Then came this clincher from Jesus: "If you want to be perfect, go, sell your possessions and give to the poor. . . . Then come, follow me" (verses 18-21, NIV).

"When the young man heard this, he went away sad, because he had great wealth" (verse 22, NIV). Morally upright in every way, but far from God! And he has lots of company today.

Sins of omission. Missing the mark. Leaving a hundred good and noble things undone!

Beneath the Surface

But David goes even deeper. He talks about *'awon*—iniquity, moral distortion, crookedness. Obviously, we're not dealing here with something you can tell people to "stop—and do it now, today!"

I have listened for countless hours to people who talk like this. I've read thousands of pages from their writings. And I've formed the impression that the sin uppermost in their minds when they admonish us to "stop sinning" has to do with sexual and other sensual indulgences. But especially with the sexual. Like the larger society around us, we seem completely fixated on sins of the flesh.

For example, when William Haynes wants to attack those who do not accept his kind of sinless perfection, he denounces a certain (unnamed) Adventist minister who, he alleges, confidently affirmed that he (the pastor) could "sleep with . . . [his] neighbor's wife and still get into the kingdom of heaven. (I can keep on sinning and still be saved.)" (William Haynes, "Fit Guests for the Wedding," *Our Firm Foundation*, July 1993, p. 9).

And Colin Standish wonders how it is possible that saints preparing for the Advent could indulge in "fornication, adultery, incest, homosexuality, theft, [and] murder" ("Issues: Sin and Transgression," *ibid.*, p. 18).

It would appear that as these gentlemen and their colleagues see it, all those who do not share their belief in sinless perfection do so because they are indulging in these kinds of activities.

Permit me, then, to be somewhat crude in order to make the following point. It may come as a surprise to some critics within Adventism to learn that most of those who oppose their perfectionist stand do not go around sleeping with other people's wives or husbands; are not indulging in premarital sex; do not go after prostitutes; are not sex molesters or perverts; do not indulge an appetite for hard pornographic literature or even *Playboy;* do not go to the movie theater, nor spend their time at home watching X-rated films or videos; alcohol and tobacco are taboo for them, and so also are caffeinated beverages of all kinds. For good measure, many of them are even practicing vegetarians.

No, these are upright men and women, maintaining the highest standards of morality and behavior. *They keep the law, if you please.* But they know that behavior is not where it's at. They understand that sin is much deeper than behavior—that it is a malady that pervades as well as *precedes* our behavior and our sinful acts. Sometimes through old age, isolation from the thoroughfares of human society, or through a gritting of the teeth, we may manage to avoid participation in sinful behavior. And this may lead us to draw the conclusion that we are somehow perfect now.

But sin is deeper, more pervasive and chronic, than some of us think. What we're looking at here is a malady buried deep in the human psyche. Isaiah probably had this in mind (he used the word *'awon* among others) when he penned his unflattering description of the human condition: "The whole head is sick, and the whole heart faint. From the sole of the foot even unto the head there is no soundness in it; but wounds, and bruises, and putrifying sores" (Isa. 1:5, 6).

That's how, apart from Jesus, we appear in God's holy eyes. Our malady is systemic. Ellen G. White describes sin as "leprosy" "deep-rooted, deadly, and impossible to be cleansed by human power" (*The Desire of Ages,* p. 266).

Long after we have ceased our willful rebellion against the Lord and been converted, the moral distortion of sin plagues us. There are shades of crookedness buried deep within us, sometimes waiting years for a certain combination of circumstances to bring them to the fore.

Through the process of sanctification (as commonly understood in Christian theology)* God works to counteract and correct this evil bent within us. "Sanctification is the work of a lifetime" because it takes time—even for God—to bring about the needed change. If we were inanimate objects or even animals, God could do it in an instant. But He has made us free moral agents, and He must engage this freedom in all attempts to develop character in us.

It is a process that entails allowing us to try . . . and fail . . . and experiment . . . and succeed—in Him. It involves disappointment and hardship, doubt and faith, fear and trust—and a thousand other factors—all under the Spirit's control. The chiseling, the polishing, the straightening, the loosening and tightening never stop. Every day as we follow on to know the Lord, the raw material of our crooked spirits becomes more pliant, more malleable. Thus the gentle Spirit molds and shapes us continually into the divine image.

What if We Die?

And what if we die before Jesus comes, or before the process ends (which, inevitably, must happen—since the process never ends this side of heaven)?

Look again at the way David, under the Spirit, puts the case. "Blessed is he whose transgressions [*pesha'*] are forgiven" (Ps. 32:1, NIV). *Our rebellion must come to an end—be put behind us, be forgiven.* I picture here a total cessation of that spirit which once led us to revolt against Heaven, to shake our fists in the face of God! Reconciliation has happened. "We have peace with God through our Lord Jesus Christ" (Rom. 5:1), and through thick or thin, as the saying goes, our loyalty remains constant to the end.

This is the picture drawn in Revelation 17:14: "These [the enemies of the cross] shall make war with the Lamb, and the Lamb shall overcome them: for he is Lord of lords, and King of kings: and they that are with him are called, and chosen, and faithful."

But as if David knew that *chatta'ah*, the missing of the mark, will continue to dog our steps until the end, he says: "Blessed is he . . .

whose sins [*chatta'ah*] are covered" (Ps. 32:1, NIV). Sin—in the sense of shortcomings—will never cease to trouble us. As long as we live in this world, interacting with people and facing new and complex situations and circumstances, we will experience shortcomings. It is not too difficult to take certain shortcomings in stride—as signs of the growing-up process. But others cause us much grief. We are not, however, to become discouraged. "There are those who have known the pardoning love of Christ, and who really desire to be children of God, yet they realize that their character is imperfect, their life faulty, and they're ready to doubt whether their hearts have been renewed by the Holy Spirit. To such I would say, Do not draw back in despair. We shall often have to bow down and weep at the feet of Jesus because of our shortcomings and mistakes; but we are not to be discouraged" (Ellen G. White, *Steps to Christ*, p. 64).

Such shortcomings and mistakes are common to the entire human family from birth to the grave, and no one who speaks the truth will deny this. They are the direct results of the congenital crookedness (*'awon*), the moral imbalance with which we were born, and against which we struggle daily.

Evidently God does not miraculously remove this problem from us. Rather, He uses it in His providence to build character in us. And though this crookedness—this natural deformity—is not a plus but rather a minus, God, says David, "does not count [it] against" the penitent child of God (Ps. 32:2, NIV). For He who reads our inmost souls understands that we are no longer in revolt against Heaven, and that those shortcomings do not constitute defiance. And God will not hold these things against those who are otherwise fully surrendered to Him. What amazing love! That's the good news of the gospel!

But like *pesha'* (rebellion), guile (*remiyyah*)—the last of the four major dimensions of sin we're considering here—must disappear completely from the Christian heart. "Blessed is the man . . . in whose spirit there is no guile" (verse 2).

The most scathing rebuke of Jesus' entire ministry was directed against the deceit, the duplicity—the guile—of the scribes and Pharisees who "do not practice what they preach" (Matt. 23:3, NIV). "Everything they do," said Jesus, "is done for men to see" (verse 5, NIV). "Woe unto you, scribes and Pharisees, hypocrites!" He thundered from the Temple courts on the eve of the cross (verses 13-29). "You snakes!" He said as He brought the withering seven-point litany to an end, "You brood of vipers! How will you escape being condemned to hell?" (verse 33, NIV).

Rebellion Versus Loyalty

David's reflection on his own problem, then, provides a much more comprehensive assessment of the human condition than we often contemplate, an assessment that even takes on eschatological significance as we come to the book of Revelation. For there the undergirding issues center around rebellion and loyalty.

On the one hand stand the beast and its followers in revolt against Heaven. On the other stands the Lamb with those who have accepted His offer of salvation and who have made peace with Him through the blood of His cross. Loyal and triumphant, they stand with Jesus on the sea of glass. "And in their mouth was found no guile: for they are without fault before the throne of God" (Rev. 14:5).

The lesson to be drawn, then, from David's prayer in Psalm 32 is that in Jesus victory is possible, that in Jesus *pesha'* (rebellion) and *remiyyah* (guile, hypocrisy, deceit) will cease. Victory in these areas of the Christian life will be complete in Jesus, for these aspects of sin are *directly and intrinsically intertwined with character.* In regard, however, to *chatta'ah* ("missing the mark") and *'awon* ("crookedness"—in the sense of natural moral deformity), God bears with completely surrendered Christians until the end. These aspects of sin do not intrinsically impinge on character and *thus do not determine our fitness or unfitness for heaven.*

And while the life of surrendered Christians will demonstrate continued growth, we will never come to the place in this life where we move beyond the reach of these infirmities. Thus our only hope of salvation—from beginning to end—is the sheer mercy and grace of God. He *covers* our *chatta'ah*, says David; and "does not count" our *'awon* against us (Ps. 32:1, 2, NIV). What a Saviour! What a God!

It is in the light of this human reality that the same Ellen G. White who holds up before us (as she should) the highest moral and spiritual standards could also write: "The closer you come to Jesus, the more faulty you will appear in your own eyes; for your vision will be clearer, and your imperfections will be seen in broad and distinct contrast to His perfect nature. This is evidence that Satan's delusions have lost their power; that the vivifying influence of the Spirit of God is arousing you.

"No deep-seated love for Jesus can dwell in the heart that does not realize its own sinfulness. The soul that is transformed by the grace of Christ will admire His divine character; *but if we do not see our own moral deformity*, it is unmistakable evidence that we have not had a view of the beauty and excellence of Christ. "The less we see to esteem in ourselves, the more we shall see to esteem in the infinite purity and loveliness of our Saviour" (*ibid.*, pp. 64, 65; italics supplied).

Unless we understand this, *we will never know the joy of assurance in Christ*. Talk to any of those who believe and preach the doctrine of absolute perfection and sinlessness, and ask them whether they have already reached that stage. The answer you receive will *not* be yes—whether these persons are 16 years old or 60 or 90. Usually, they fudge. And why? Because they find it difficult to lie.

Think logically, then. If at 60—even at 90—we have not yet arrived, then when?

I have presented the subject of this chapter the way I have, not because I enjoy in any way coming short of the mark, but because that is the way it is *with all of us*. Reality is not always as tidy as we would like it to be. But we must face up to it and speak the truth. Only when we understand the various dimensions of sin will we see the underlying harmony in the apparently conflicting statements of Scripture.

With the definitions and explanations before us as presented in this chapter, we can now understand how the same John can say, on the one hand, that "no one who lives" in Christ "keeps on sinning" (1 John 3:6, NIV) and, on the other hand, that "if we say we have no sin, we deceive ourselves, and the truth is not in us" (1 John 1:8).

---

* As has been pointed out again and again, the word "sanctify" in the Bible does not fall into the neat slot we have made for it in Christian theology. In the Bible, sanctification represents both a present *and* a future experience for the Christian—both a gift and a goal. (See Acts 20:32; Rom. 15:16; 1 Cor. 1:2; Rom. 6:19; 1 Thess. 4:3.)

Chapter 7

CORPORATE REPENTANCE:
Who Demands It?

Today there is deep anger among our concerned brethren and also among our disaffected brethren—anger and frustration arising from what they perceive as a stubborn and intransigent church ignoring repeated calls to repent.

And you'd be frustrated too, whoever you are—and perhaps even a little bit angry—if you shared the sense of urgency implied in the following statement by Wieland and Short: "The cleansing of the sanctuary can never be complete until the 1888 incident of our history is fully understood and the underlying spiritual problem solved" (*1888 Re-examined*, p. 4).

It is this perceived connection between impending events in heaven and the actions of the church on earth that has produced their calls for "corporate repentance." Without this repentance the church will remain lukewarm, "ill with spiritual disease that can be traced to 1888." We *must* repent. "A failure to do so invokes upon ourselves the guilt of previous generations" (*ibid.*, p. 5).

Sometimes I find it difficult to nail down exactly what these brethren have in mind when they talk about "corporate repentance." What form should it take, for example? The situation is murky.

In his latest book on the subject, Wieland makes a conscious effort, I think, to fill out some of the details. Building his argument around the message to the church of Laodicea (Rev. 3:14-22), he notes that the divine missive is directed to the "angel" of the Laodicean church. This "angel," he says, includes "Sabbath school leaders; academy, college, and university teachers; local elders; deacons; Pathfinder leaders; pastors; local and union conference leaders; and of course General Conference leadership—all who guide the church" (Robert J. Wieland, *Corporate Repentance*, pp. 13, 14).

As I understand Wieland, these people must take the lead in the act of corporate repentance, setting an example for the rest of the church. It will not be simple, he admits, with the "complex machinery" of the church getting in the way of the working of the Spirit. And he seems to sense what he calls "the practical problem" of a multi-million member church repenting (*ibid.*, p. 113).

But if Wieland and his colleagues are not sure about procedures, they are quite clear about the need for such repentance. "After 6,000 years of waiting, the Saviour makes His last plea," Wieland says. "This has gone unheeded for well over a century" (*ibid.*, p. 9). Never has the Lord had a more difficult problem to solve than the "lukewarmness of the human leadership of His last-day remnant church" (*ibid.*, p. 11). The message that God sent us in 1888 was "a distinct, unique presentation of righteousness by faith" that goes "far beyond the message by the same name . . . [in] the popular churches" (*ibid.*, p. 32). But Adventist church leaders have suppressed it, kept it from the people, and have "sharply contested for over 40 years" the topic of corporate repentance (*ibid.*, pp. 40, 17). What we need now is to *"demonstrate our repentance by recovering the message we lost"* (*ibid.*, p. 41).

Far from backing away in the face of what he sees as the church's resistance to corporate repentance, Wieland makes the stakes even higher—or is it deeper? What's called for, he says, is "a Day-of-Atonement repentance" (*ibid.*, pp. 58, 65), a "deeper repentance," arising from the consciousness of a "deeper level of guilt." It is a repentance that is to lead, not merely to forgiveness, but to the "blotting out" of sin (*ibid.*, p. 66). This repentance by Laodicea is to be "unique in world history" (*ibid.*, p. 67).

Becoming even more ominous, Wieland contends that this "deeper phase of repentance" must include *"repenting of sins that we may not have committed, but which we would have committed if we had the opportunity"* (*ibid.*, p. 69; italics supplied). And he informs us—without bothering to support it—that "our potential for sin is already recorded in the books of heaven" (*ibid.*, p. 70). And as if to make the situation even more hopeless for us, Wieland asserts, incredibly, that "only a Perfect Person can experience a perfect and complete repentance" (*ibid.*, p. 75).*

It is clear from their persistence on this theme that corporate repentance has *not* yet been offered by the church to *their* satisfaction. Nor to the satisfaction of Heaven. Note this remarkable statement: "The practical results of the investigative judgment will require that the remnant church, before the time of final victory, come to see the truth of the message of its history, and recognize Jones' and Waggoner's work from 1888-1896 for its true value, the 'beginning' of the latter rain and the loud cry" (*1888 Reexamined*, p. 117).

Think about it! With millions going down to Christless graves every day; millions physically starving to death around the world; thousands upon thousands dying (as I write) in the former Yugoslavia and in Sudan of hunger, exposure, and naked brutality; with the nations in turmoil over the most horrendous moral and social developments in the history of the world; indeed, with the whole creation groaning for redemption, the great God of the universe has stayed His hand of blessing for more than 100 years because He is waiting for modern Adventists to confess their rejection of the message brought by two young preachers more than a century ago! "All things are being held up" for lack of corporate repentance on the part of the church (*Corporate Repentance*, p. 64).

Sounds incredible, doesn't it?

Charges of a Cover-up

But however shrill the cries for corporate repentance might sound to most of us, these brethren consider their responsibility to be the most urgent task committed to humans since the coming of John the Baptist. And they see the refusal of church leaders to take them seriously as nothing short of a conspiracy to cover up this vital period of our history. "The findings of this essay [Wieland and Short's book] suggest there has been some grave official misunderstanding of vital Seventh-day Adventist history. There is evidence that truth concerning the latter rain of the Holy Spirit and the loud cry of Revelation 18 has been distorted *and even covered up*" (*1888 Re-examined*, p. 3; italics supplied). This is a systemic problem for the church, as these two brethren see it—a kind of "denominational neurosis" (*ibid.*, p. 89).

Through statements like these, we are given to believe that the Holy Spirit has been held back for more than 100 years because the church has not come clean on what happened in 1888.

Perhaps there is something I'm missing here or don't quite understand, but I find this position incomprehensible. It is so esoteric, so provincial, that I have extreme difficulty relating to it.

No one should assume for a moment that I am uninterested in what happened in 1888. That episode was truly a theological watershed for us. And there are, indeed, many lessons still to learn from it. *This point is not in dispute here.* But I'm genuinely astonished by the preoccupation with those events on the part of some of our people. Indeed, in many cases it appears to have gone beyond preoccupation to a sort of cultlike fixation, completely unintelligible to a new generation of Adventists.

What would objective Bible students not of our faith think about such theological quaintness? More important, what picture does it paint of God's character? Is it not that of a God who holds His anger forever? I wonder if this might not be among the most specious strains of "legalism" ever foisted upon a people *in the name of righteousness by faith.* Hear Wieland and Short again: "Full confession" by the church for the rejection of the 1888 message "was never made." And although the actual participants of the 1888 conference have all died, "that does not mean those 'record books of heaven' are automatically cleansed. They record corporate sin as well as personal sin" (*ibid.*, p. 4).

In short, the church remains guilty of grave sin.

Who Requires It?

The fundamental question to ask in connection with the call for "corporate repentance" is Who requires it of us?

Arnold Wallenkampf, in a little book he wrote to coincide with the one hundredth anniversary of the historic Minneapolis

General Conference session, takes dead aim at the idea of corporate repentance. "The notion of corporate sin and consequent corporate guilt is foreign to God's dealings with man," he insists. God made us free moral agents. "Sin, with resultant guilt, stems from the exercise of free moral choice and rests on personal accountability before God" (*What Every Adventist Should Know About 1888*, p. 53).

Giving every evidence of having heard the proponents of corporate repentance, Wallenkampf couched his position in language too clear to be misunderstood. "In the matter of sin, God does not deal with groups of people or with committees. He does not hold a committee as such responsible for the actions that the committee takes. God deals with individuals. Even though a committee, or a church through its delegated representatives, may have made a wrong decision, in taking notice of their corporate decision God still holds only the respective individuals who constituted that committee responsible for the votes they cast" (*ibid.*). Moreover, Wallenkampf says that "no vote was ever taken" on whether to accept or reject the message brought by Jones and Waggoner to the 1888 conference (*ibid.*, p. 54). But "even if a vote had been cast by the assembly and the majority had voted against the 1888 message, the sin committed still would not have constituted corporate sin, but would be sin on the part of each person voting against it" (*ibid.*, p. 55).

To my knowledge, no Adventist theologian has made a bolder case against corporate confession than Wallenkampf has done here. Are his statements too strong, however? Has he overstated the case?

It seems to me that numerous examples might be cited from the Old Testament for what looks very much like corporate repentance. In the time of Hezekiah, for example, the king said to the assembled spiritual leaders of Israel: "Consecrate yourselves. . . . For our fathers have been unfaithful and have done evil in the sight of the Lord. . . . Therefore the wrath of the Lord was against Judah and Jerusalem, and He has made them an object of terror . . . , as you see with your own eyes. . . . Now it is in my heart to make a covenant with the Lord . . . , that His burning anger may turn away from us. My sons, do not be negligent now, for the Lord has chosen you to stand before Him" (2 Chron. 29:5-11, NASB). And the Levites responded (verses 12-16).

A time of confession and reconsecration also took place during the time of Josiah after the book of the law was discovered in the Temple (see 2 Chron. 34:14-30).

And the prophet Joel admonished: "Blow a trumpet in Zion, consecrate a fast, proclaim a solemn assembly, gather the people, sanctify the congregation, assemble the elders. . . . Let the priests, the Lord's ministers, weep between the porch and the altar, and let them say, 'Spare Thy people, O Lord'" (Joel 2:15-17, NASB).

If these were not examples of what might be called corporate repentance, they certainly came very close, wouldn't you say?

And in regard to Wallenkampf's strong insistence on the inculpability of committees, I also have a little trouble. I cannot imagine the church assembled in general session, for example, taking an action palpably contrary to biblical principles without feeling some sense of corporate responsibility when evidence of the fact is brought to its attention. Clearly it will not do to distribute culpability for the action merely to the individuals taking the vote.

But the fact that Wallenkampf somewhat overstated the case does not damage, for me, the basic thrust of his argument. One question to ask is whether the corporateness of the Christian church today is equivalent to the corporateness of the tightly knit, geographically confined theocracy of ancient Israel. And is there any significance to the fact that the New Testament offers us not a single authentic example of general corporate confession?

Way back in Old Testament times, as Wallenkampf points out, God had already enunciated the principle of individual accountability! "The soul who sins is the one who will die. The son will not share the guilt of the father, nor will the father share the guilt of the son. The righteousness of the righteous man will be credited to him, and the wickedness of the wicked will be charged against him" (Eze. 18:20, NIV).

The Specific Issue

However, regardless of where you stand on the question as I have developed it thus far, the essential thing to remember is that in this chapter we are not dealing with the general question of corporate repentance, as such. We are not even dealing with the message to Laodicea. That message must stand as a constant warning to the church against spiritual arrogance and pride. It is an accurate description by the Holy Spirit of our condition. But that is not what we're discussing here.

The question of concern here, rather, is whether the Seventh-day Adventist Church has been called by the Lord to repent for what happened (or did not happen) in 1888. That's the issue.

And the essential thing to note about the examples of corporate repentance in the Old Testament is that *every such call was initiated by some inspired leader or prophet.*

What inspired support do today's proponents of corporate repentance offer for their position? One would have expected that on a matter as vital as this one obviously is to those who urge it—that its proponents would have marshaled in its defense the strongest possible statements they could find from the Bible or the Spirit of Prophecy. But anyone who takes the time to examine the arguments presented in defense of this notion will be surprised by the absence of any credible evidence for it.

In the crucial first chapter of their book *1888 Re-examined*, Wieland and Short raise the question: "Why re-examine our past?" How helpful would have been a ringing quote from Ellen White at this point! But the best they found was this one: "The sin committed in what took place at Minneapolis remains on the record books of heaven, *registered against the names of those who resisted* light, and it will remain upon the record until full confession is made, and the transgressors stand in full humility before God" (letter 19d, 1892; cited in *Ellen G. White Manuscript Releases*, vol. 2, p. 57, and *1888 Re-examined*, p. 4).

But notice that the statement was penned in 1892, more than 100 years ago. It related to a specific historical incident, and, although not mentioning names, had in mind specific individuals, as

Wallenkampf notes (*What Every Adventist Should Know About 1888*, pp. 55, 56)—most likely those leaders involved in the 1888 discussions and debate. Is it really rational to think that the warning expressed way back then should be given *unlimited application* for the future—to generations yet unborn?

M. L. Andreasen once told an amusing story about himself that bears repeating in this connection. While a bachelor, he came upon a statement in the writings of Ellen White that read: "You eat too much." Convicted, he cut back on personal consumption. Some months later he was startled to run across the same statement, its message unchanged: "You eat too much." He cut back again. After a few months, as chance would have it, he happened upon the very statement one more time, and there it was, reading just as it always had, confronting the now virtually starving bachelor with its clear-cut message: "You eat too much." Andreasen said he almost killed himself before he came to his senses.

Clearly, time and place have to be taken into consideration when interpreting any document—and the writings of Ellen G. White are no exception. Once penned, the words remain written. But must we think that in every case they apply—forever—in their literal, primary meaning?

Some time ago I watched on television a debate among a multi-ethnic group of high school seniors. When one Black student tried to remind his White colleagues for the umpteenth time how they and their forebears had mistreated him, one White young lady couldn't take it any longer. "I'm only *17 years of age!*" she said in deep frustration. "*I haven't done anything to you!*"

Human society cannot move forward unless people are prepared to leave the past behind. Wherever a people or a society find this impossible, there is bloodshed and backwardness. Look at the Middle East today. Look at Northern Ireland. Look at Yugoslavia. Look at Sudan.

Yet this is what people like Wieland and Short wish on us. "Why pay such attention to the tragic past?" they ask. "Why not forget it and go 'forward' from where we are now?" (*1888 Re-examined*, p. 6).

Yes indeed! Why not?

But their own answer goes the opposite direction. Misapplying the reference, they note that "Ellen White . . . reminds us that there is terrible danger in forgetting the past" (*ibid.*).

Notice that they do not quote her directly on this one. If they did, everyone would notice that what she said was the following: "In reviewing our past history, having traveled over every step of advance to our present standing, I can say, Praise God! As I see what the Lord has wrought, I am filled with astonishment, and with confidence in Christ as leader. We have nothing to fear for the future, except as we shall forget the way the Lord has led us, and His teaching in our past history" (*Life Sketches*, p. 196).

So the looking back that she envisioned was for the purpose of building confidence in God and learning lessons for the future. She was not advocating a fixation with the past, a constant dwelling on it. That was not her point. She would heartily concur in the sentiments of the apostle, as healthy for a church as for individuals: "Forgetting what lies behind and reaching forward to what lies ahead, I press on toward the goal for the prize of the upward call of God in Christ Jesus" (Phil. 3:13, 14, NASB).

Where would the United States be today if it went digging up the issues behind the Civil War (which, incidentally, wasn't that much earlier than Minneapolis) and continued fighting it all over again? What would be the relations between Great Britain and America today if they would insist on keeping alive the irritants that provoked the American War of Independence?

If human governments can bury the hatchet, letting bygones be bygones, then why do we imagine that God will not do the same with His people?

"How often shall my brother sin against me and I forgive him?" Peter asked of the Lord. "Up to seven times?" But Jesus answered, "I do not say to you, up to seven times, but up to seventy times seven" (Matt. 18:21, 22, NASB). If God expects us to be forgiving to that extent, will He do less?

Wieland's book on corporate repentance includes passages that are truly commendable and positive. I recall reading in several places throughout the book appeals to reflect Jesus in His love and compassion. "Such an experience," he says, "will transform the church into a dynamo of love." "Corporate and denominational repentance is the whole church experiencing Christlike love and empathy for all for whom He died" (*Corporate Repentance*, p. 142).

But a knowledge of the author's total agenda makes one hesitant to sound a lusty amen too quickly, because earlier he had raised the following question about that same Jesus whose love we must reflect: "Could Jesus accuse people of a crime when they were innocent?" Incredibly, Wieland's answer is yes (*ibid.*, p. 90).

Jesus did that, Wieland claimed, when He charged the Jewish leaders of His time with the murder of Zechariah the priest (Matt. 23:35), which had occurred 800 years earlier. "Jesus was not unfair," Wieland contends, once "we see the principle of corporate guilt" (*ibid.*, pp. 91, 92).

In the same way, we are guilty for what our forefathers did in 1888 and must repent. Even children understand the principle, he says. "Although it is . . . [the child's] hand that steals from the cookie jar . . . it's his bottom that gets spanked" (*ibid.*, p. 93).

But go back and read Matthew 23 for yourself and see if Jesus believed that He was talking to "innocent" people, as Wieland claimed. Follow Him as He cataloged in the most graphic language of His entire ministry the crimes and hypocrisies of a nation on the very edge of its probationary limits. As God had done a thousand times before, He would yet send them special messengers at the eleventh hour. But "some of them you will kill and crucify," Jesus said, and "scourge" and "persecute" (Matt. 23:34, NASB). It was such murderous acts and schemes that brought the guilt of former generations down on the Jewish leaders and people. It was their treacherous spirit that led Jesus to identify them with the ancient murderers of Zechariah the priest. Today, we'd make the same linkage between violent contemporary Nazi skinheads and their diabolic hero of yesteryear. But should we stigmatize the entire German nation? Not if they view these skinheads with the same repugnance and contempt that we do.

If we take Jesus' words, directed to those in the throes of perpetrating the most murderous acts against Him and His followers, as somehow depicting His attitude toward honest Christians who are genuinely trying to the best of their ability to proclaim His name in the world, then we turn truth on its head and confound all logic.

This fixation for 1888 is doing strange things to us. Some among us are busily making this period of our history repugnant to large numbers of contemporary Adventists, investing it with a cultish shadow, thereby scuttling any possibility that this generation will fully appreciate the lessons it should learn from this episode in our past. This is a gross disservice to our denominational history and to the glorious cause of righteousness by faith.

Let us say it without fear and without ambiguity: The God portrayed by those calling for corporate repentance after 100 years is not the God of the Bible. "Who is a God like you, who pardons sin and forgives the transgression of the remnant of his inheritance? You do not stay angry forever but delight to show mercy" (Micah 7:18, NIV). "'For I know the plans I have for you,' declares the Lord, 'plans to prosper you and not to harm you, plans to give you hope and a future'" (Jer. 29:11, NIV). "If thou, O Lord, shouldest mark iniquities, . . . who shall stand? But there is forgiveness with thee" (Ps. 130:3, 4).

How can we bear joyful witness for the Lord with a perpetual dark cloud of guilt hanging over our heads? What morbid satisfaction can possibly come from this joyless doctrine? How can people be attracted to a religion like this? How can our young people be expected ever to take up and carry forward a message of fear and guilt, and one, moreover, that makes absolutely no sense to them?

Could it be that one reason for the continuance of the agitation over corporate repentance among us springs from our own insecurity—as leaders and as a people? Could it be that there lies deep within our psyches a latent fear that these brethren may *perhaps just be right, after all?* Is this the depth of our theology? Is this the level of our understanding of God's nature and character?

I think we should make it clear as a church that the idea of corporate repentance as promulgated by some among us *has no merit.* It has not a single shred of support in the writings of Ellen G. White.

Those who piously seek to manipulate God's people by means of guilt are following the same pattern that leads to a Jonestown or a Waco. They may be further up the line from a Jim Jones or a David Koresh, but it's the same continuum.

These are strong words, I know, and I write them kindly. But perhaps the time has come for them—if perchance we can rescue those on the verge of surrendering their God-given independence and judgment to a group of deluded, self-appointed gurus. We cannot stand silent while many of our unsuspecting people fall into the trap of perfectionistic legalism foisted upon them by the piety and dogmatism of a few frustrated and sometimes disgruntled brethren.

If Jonestown and Waco tell us anything, it is that we ought to be exceedingly suspicious of all who ask us to accept any idea or teaching solely upon their say-so. And that exactly is the foundation on which the idea of corporate repentance vis à vis 1888 rests. Waco, in particular, has shown that a multitude of "proof texts"—whether from the Bible or the Spirit of Prophecy—do not, in themselves, constitute a badge of orthodoxy. Regardless of the piety or apparent sincerity of the messenger, we owe it to God and to ourselves to *think!*

The advocates of corporate repentance could not possibly substantiate their position vis à vis 1888 from Scripture. And we should not expect them to—for obvious reasons. But neither can they do it from the writings of Ellen G. White—and we *should* expect them to—for obvious reasons. I read Wieland's new book, *Corporate Repentance*, looking for just one thing—evidence from an inspired source that the church has a duty to repent today for the rejection by church leaders in 1888 of the message of Jones and Waggoner. *Surely at this late hour and after years of research on this topic, Wieland has found something now,* I thought. *Why else would he write a new book on the subject?* But I searched in vain. *There was none—not a shred.*

From Ellen G. White—A Positive Message

If Ellen White had any sense of the kind of urgency some of our brethren today attach to this issue, she certainly did not show it. Had this been an issue of any magnitude with her, what better place to have emphasized it than in her last written statement? But we find nothing of the kind there. On the contrary, her theme in that last statement was one of victory, of joy, and of assurance in Jesus (see *Testimonies to Ministers*, pp. 516-520).

Here are a few sample excerpts.

"Dear Friends: The Lord has given me a message for you, and not for you only, but also for other faithful souls who are *troubled by doubts and fears regarding their acceptance by the Lord Jesus Christ. His word to you is, 'Fear not*: for I have redeemed thee, I have called thee by thy name; thou art mine.' *You desire to please the Lord, and you can do this by believing His promises*" (italics supplied).

"*The joy of Christ in the soul is worth everything.* 'Then are they glad,' because they are privileged to rest in the arms of everlasting love" (italics supplied).

"Do not talk of your inefficiency and your defects. When despair would seem to be sweeping over your soul, look to Jesus, saying, He lives to make intercession for me. *Forget the things that are behind, and believe the promise,* 'I will come to you,' and 'abide with you'" (italics supplied).

"*I rejoice in the bright prospects of the future, and so may you. Be cheerful, and praise the Lord for His loving-kindness.* That which you cannot understand, commit to Him. He loves you and pities your every weakness. He 'hath blessed us with all spiritual blessings in heavenly places in Christ.' It would not satisfy the heart of the Infinite One to give those who love His Son a lesser blessing than He gives His Son" (italics supplied).

"Christ's love for His children is as tender as it is strong. And it is stronger than death; for He died to purchase our salvation, and to make us one with Him, mystically and eternally one. So strong is His love that it controls all His powers, and employs the vast resources of heaven in doing His people good."

These are the hopeful words from the Lord's messenger on the eve of her death. What a contrast to the cheerless preachments and threats of doom we hear from certain quarters today! Christian history is replete with pious, self-appointed prophets whom God did not send. The word of the Lord through Jeremiah is relevant for our times: "Then the Lord said to me, 'The prophets are prophesying lies in my name. I have not sent them or appointed them or spoken to them. They are prophesying to you false visions . . . and the delusions of their own minds'" (Jer. 14:14, NIV).

Corporate repentance. Who demands it of us? I make bold to say it: Not the Lord!

---

* Note the capitalized letters in "Perfect Person." To whom is Wieland referring here? What does he mean?

Chapter 8

WHAT DOES GOD REQUIRE?

In Revelation 14 John pictures the 144,000 standing victorious on Mount Zion with Jesus the Lamb. These had "not been defiled with women," it says, "for they have kept themselves chaste" (verse 4, NASB). They represent the "first fruits unto God and to the Lamb. *And in their mouth was found no guile: for they are without fault before the throne of God*" (verses 1, 4, 5).

What does this passage mean? Does God require of the final generation a certain standard or quality of righteousness not expected of previous generations of believers? When we get to heaven, will members of earth's last generation be able to claim in the presence of the redeemed of previous generations that their own righteousness was of a higher quality than that of the rest?

This is the question before us now.

Absolute Perfection

For Andreasen and those who follow his lead today, the answer to these questions is an unqualified yes. In fact, one of Andreasen's chief underlying concerns in his approach to the doctrine of the sanctuary was to emphasize the need for "absolute perfection" on the part of the final generation of Christians. God's very vindication rests on this achievement, claimed Andreasen. Through Christ's final ministration in the heavenly sanctuary, God must demonstrate that the perfection Christ achieved was not unique but repeatable in His end-time saints (see Adams, *The Sanctuary Doctrine*, pp. 179, 180).

In developing his position on this point, Andreasen called attention to Philippians 3:12, 15. In verse 12, Paul indicated he had not yet obtained perfection: *"Not that I have already . . . become perfect,* but I press on . . ."* (NASB). In verse 15, however, he claimed perfection for himself and others: "Let us therefore, *as many as are perfect,* have this attitude" (NASB).

Explaining this apparent contradiction, Andreasen noted that the perfection referred to in verse 15 is "relative perfection." That kind of perfection Paul and the believers of his day had achieved. But not the "absolute perfection" of verse 12, said Andreasen.

"But will any ever reach that stage [of absolute perfection]?" asked Andreasen. "We believe so," he answered, pointing his readers to the description of the 144,000 given in Revelation 14:4, 5 (*The Book of Hebrews,* p. 467). According to Andreasen, Jesus' second coming cannot take place until that level of perfection has been achieved by the final generation.[1]

This righteousness, said Andreasen, is produced in connection with the cleansing of the sanctuary, the final phase of Christ's atonement. It is an understanding of righteousness "distinctly Adventist" (Andreasen, *Letters,* "The Atonement," pp. 11-14).

In their preaching of this kind of righteousness, says Wieland [echoing Andreasen], Jones and Waggoner went beyond Luther. "They built upon this foundation [the one laid by the Reformers] a grand edifice of truth that is unique and distinctly Seventh-day Adventist" (*The 1888 Message,* p. 38).

"Not that the Lord has prohibited former generations from attaining 'unto the measure of the stature of the fulness of Christ,'" Wieland notes, "but simply that no former generation has in fact ever attained to the condition that Revelation postulates for the bride of Christ—His 'bride has made herself ready' (Rev. 19:7, RSV)" (*ibid.,* p. 111).

Though the proponents of sinless perfectionism may shy away from the expression "absolute perfection," the concept they espouse vis-à-vis sinless perfection is virtually identical to that held by Andreasen and Ballenger.

"God cannot permit the sinner to enter heaven if even the slightest remnant of sin mars his character, because the admission of even an amount the size of a tiny seed would grow until it again contaminated the universe" (*ibid.*, p. 87).

That statement is correct, of course, if we're talking about sin as *pesha'* (rebellion, defiance, intransigence, sacrilege, revolt, independence from God, willful transgression). Or if we're talking about sin as *remiyyah* (guile, deceit, duplicity). But when we understand sin also as *chatta'ah* (missing the mark) or as *'awon* (moral distortion) [see chapter 6], then Wieland's statement becomes at once meaningless and misleading.

The message of 1888, according to these reform Adventists, focused on this unique concept of righteousness, a brand-new emphasis unknown in previous theology—"a unique spiritual nutriment that leads to 'obedience to all the commandments of God'" (*1888 Re-examined*, p. 53).[2] The 1888 message, according to Wieland and Short, "was not a mere re-emphasis of the doctrines of Martin Luther and John Wesley, nor even of the Adventist pioneers. . . . [Rather,] it was the 'beginning' of a more mature concept of the 'everlasting gospel' than had been clearly perceived by any previous generation" (*ibid.*, p. 55).

I have to say here that as I pored over hundreds of pages in the writings of these brethren, I kept asking myself, "What on earth is troubling these people so? What do they want the church to do?"

Boiled down to its essence, their idea is that just as Jesus, in sinful human flesh, lived a sinless life of absolute perfection, so can we—so must we—through His atonement for us in the heavenly sanctuary. We must be absolutely perfect. Only when the church reaches that state will Jesus come. This, they hold, was the message of 1888. *We can stop sinning. We can be perfect.* And this is God's requirement for the final generation of believers.

The Position of Ellen G. White

As most of us know, the approach of those who espouse absolute perfection and sinlessness is based almost solely on the writings of Ellen G. White. I must, therefore, of necessity, touch on the way she dealt with this issue. I will not attempt a full-scale discussion of her position here, however, *since my purpose in this chapter is the narrow one of discovering whether a higher spiritual standard is required of us today than of previous generations.*

George Knight in his book *The Pharisee's Guide to Perfect Holiness* has again done the church a service in his careful pursuit of a resolution to the seemingly conflicting statements in Ellen G. White on perfection and sinless living. What he does there is not exactly what I'm attempting here. But the two approaches are obviously related. Let me, therefore, touch on a few of the points he developed as a way of getting to my own.

Knight begins by boldly admitting that Ellen White did espouse the idea of character perfection. She did so, he contends, not merely in relation to forensic justification by faith (clothed in Christ's own perfection), but also in terms of "what God does *in* us through the dynamic power of the Holy Spirit" (p. 171).

In support of this point, Knight presents a list of strong statements from Ellen White, of which the following are representative.

"The Lord requires perfection from His redeemed family. He calls for perfection in character-building" (*The SDA Bible Commentary*, Ellen G. White Comments, vol. 5, p. 1085; cited in *Pharisee's Guide*, p. 171). "We should cultivate every faculty to the highest degree of perfection. . . . Moral perfection is required of all. Never should we lower the standard of righteousness in order to accommodate inherited or cultivated tendencies to wrong doing" (*Christ's Object Lessons*, p. 330; cited in *Pharisee's Guide*, p. 171). Ellen White, in fact, goes so far as to say that "imperfection of character is sin" (*Christ's Object Lessons*, p. 330).

Knight also calls attention to Ellen White's emphasis on our becoming like Christ in character. She said: "The very image of God is to be reproduced in humanity. The honor of God, the honor of Christ, is involved in the perfection of the character of His people" (*The Desire of Ages*, p. 671; cited in *Pharisee's Guide*, p. 173).

These are strong statements, and there are more where they came from. But Knight notes that there are counterbalancing statements as well.

"[Christ] is a perfect and holy example, given for us to imitate. *We cannot equal the pattern*; but we shall not be approved of God if we do not copy it and, according to the ability which God has given, resemble it" (*Testimonies*, vol. 2, p. 549; cited in *Pharisee's Guide*, p. 174; italics supplied).

In another place she wrote: "We can never equal the pattern; but we may imitate and resemble it according to our ability" (*Review and Herald*, Feb. 5, 1895, p. 81; cited in *Pharisee's Guide*, p. 174). "In another connection," said Knight, "she flatly claimed that 'no one is [ultimately] perfect but Jesus'" (*The Pharisee's Guide*, p. 174; quoting Ellen G. White manuscript 24, 1892, in *1888 Materials*, p. 1089).

And there is much more in Ellen White's writings along this vein. We could wish that she would have been more systematic in her presentation of the issue. But much as that would have helped us today in our struggle to understand what God requires of us, it would have been impossible for her to speak or write with the kind of mathematical precision we expect. No one who writes or speaks extensively can do it that way. Inevitably, there will be contradictions—whether real or apparent.

On this issue it has been my observation that we often misunderstand Ellen White by not paying sufficient attention to the historical context in which she wrote and the live issues that she was addressing.

Let me give one such example.

She once wrote: "Let none deceive themselves with the belief that they can become holy while willfully violating one of God's requirements. The commission of a known sin silences the witnessing voice of the Spirit and separates the soul from God" (*The Great Controversy*, p. 472).

Some among us would immediately pull a statement like that out of its historical-theological context, making it serve their perfectionistic agenda, and use it against their fellow contemporary brothers and sisters.

But the careful reader will try to remember that she was not writing in a vacuum. She was not using words that apply equally and indiscriminately to everybody, whether inside or outside the Adventist Church. The expenditure of just a few minutes to examine the context will show that she was writing against the backdrop of a kind of "sanctification now [1880s-1890s] gaining prominence in the religious world" (*ibid.*, p. 471). It was a kind of sanctification characterized by "a disregard for the law of God." "Its advocates teach that sanctification is an instantaneous work, by which, through faith alone, they attain to perfect holiness. 'Only believe,'" they said. "No further effort" is required. Believers are "released from obligation to keep the commandments" (*ibid.*).

This is the situation that called forth Ellen White's remarks in regard to holiness. She referred to this philosophy as an "ensnaring doctrine of faith without works." Then comes her statement: "Let none deceive themselves . . . that they can become holy while willfully violating one of God's requirements" (*ibid.*, p. 472). To turn around and use this statement against Adventists already striving, by God's grace, to obey and teach the Ten Commandments is to turn her admonition on its head. It is inappropriate, mischievous, and even, perhaps, cruel. For by forcing the statement into a contrived context, the expression "while willfully violating one of God's requirements" is thereby removed from the specificity of the Ten Commandments and given a universality that engenders feelings of helplessness and free-floating guilt.

There is perhaps a sense in which we might say that the statement applies to all of us. But before we make any personal application, it is critically important to know *who* her primary target was and *what* the primary issue was. When we do this, taking note of the false theory of sanctification and holiness that she was addressing, we will also be in a better position to understand the following statement, which appears in the same context: "And the claim to be without sin is, in itself, evidence that he who makes this claim is far from holy. It is because he has no true conception of the infinite purity and holiness of God" (*ibid.*, p. 473).

Incidentally, making the application of that last statement after due consideration of the context, we may see it as a kind of double entendre—having two interpretations, cutting both ways. In other words, it would apply first to those nineteenth-century antinomians, but second to the perfectionists of our own time.

I've used the foregoing extended example because of what I see as a widespread tendency among many simply to ignore some of the relevant Ellen White statements and wrest others out of their proper context. Every time we find apparently conflicting statements in the Spirit of Prophecy, we should take it as a clue to be particularly vigilant, to pay closer attention.

Knight, having done so, was led to the conclusion that for her the fundamental concern in regard to perfection was not with the multitudinous bits and pieces of our behavior, but rather "with the great motivating principle of love that shapes and transforms" the tendencies of our lives "through God's grace" (*Pharisee's Guide*, p. 180). This conclusion ties in well with her statement that "character is revealed, not by occasional good deeds and occasional misdeeds, but by the tendency of the habitual words and acts" (*Steps to Christ*, pp. 57, 58).

Ellen White's apparent contradictions on this issue will not go away just because George Knight or I or someone else has written about them. They are there to stay. What each of us needs to remember is that what we view as contradictions represents God's way of speaking to the different personalities and needs of His diverse children.

Ann Burke expressed it well. "It is unfortunate," she said, "that, because of our temperaments, overconscientious believers often single out strong statements probably intended for careless Christians [the sanctified antinomians of Mrs. White's time are a case in point]. They whip themselves with these statements, while careless church members find false security in those [statements] no doubt meant to comfort the oversensitive" (Ann Cunningham Burke, "The Adventist Elephant," *Adventist Review*, Aug. 27, 1987, p. 9; cited in *Pharisee's Guide*, p. 182).

The ideas that I'm trying to share here in terms of God's requirements for us as reflected in Ellen White's writings have exceedingly practical implications for every Adventist Christian. One can become extremely depressed and discouraged if one pursues a one-sided reading of the Bible or Ellen White. It's like reading a medical book and feeling as if one had all the symptoms described in it. So my attempt to arrive at a balanced approach is not being done to win a theoretical argument—not by any means. Rather, I consider it crucial to our spiritual and psychological well-being to have a correct conception of what God has done for us and what He expects of us.

The people I most admire—whether within the Adventist Church or outside of it, the people about whom my heart unconsciously says "I wish I could be like him/like her"—are those who never dwell on the subject of perfection or sinlessness. Instead, unconsciously, they live out before me what I see as the very incarnation of Jesus' life. Their thoughtfulness, their kindness, their sense of humor, and their down-to-earth goodness attract me. I feel comfortable in their presence. I'm never embarrassed or put down. These are the people who show me what it means to be a Christian. I think they are the ones who fit this splendid description of perfection: "Love is the basis of godliness. . . . When self is merged in Christ, love springs forth spontaneously. *The completeness of Christian character is attained when the impulse to help and bless others springs constantly from within—when the sunshine of heaven fills the heart and is revealed in the countenance*" (*Christ's Object Lessons*, p. 384; italics supplied).

This, I think, is the kind of incarnational ministry, the kind of spontaneous winsomeness, that God is looking for.

The "Character of Christ" Statement

But I know that this segment on Ellen White's position will not be complete without an assessment of a certain oft-quoted statement in *Christ's Object Lessons* dealing with the character of Christ being perfectly reproduced in His people before He can come.

Some time ago, after years of hearing the statement flung into heated discussions of perfection or quoted piously by those who understand it a certain way, I undertook to study it for myself within its own context. Let me share with you, in case you missed it, the editorial I wrote in the *Adventist Review* describing what I'd found (see Adams, "What Did She Mean?" *Adventist Review*, Sept. 3, 1992, p. 4).

Here is the statement, followed by the rest of the editorial, slightly altered: "*Christ is waiting with longing desire for the manifestation of Himself in His church. When the character of Christ shall be perfectly reproduced in His people, then He will come to claim them as His own*" (*Christ's*

Object Lessons, p. 69; italics supplied).

"This statement, a key text of Adventists who advocate the absolute sinless perfection of God's last-day people before Jesus can come, is one of the most widely misunderstood in the writings of Ellen G. White. The popular understanding of it creates the picture of a church turned inward upon itself in perpetual navel-gazing and self-flagellation, struggling to achieve the perfect reproduction of the character of Christ—whatever the imagination considers that to be—so that Jesus can come.

"But what was Mrs. White trying to say?

"The best way to understand a statement whose author is no longer available for personal clarification is to examine it in context. Fortunately for us, the above statement, unlike many others that give us trouble, comes with considerable context around it. The chapter in which it occurs centers on Jesus' parable of the seed (see Mark 4:26-29), a parable Mrs. White applies to the processes of growth and fruit-bearing in the Christian life.

"Running through the chapter is a movement from seed-sowing to growth to harvest—and then back again. The progress is not always smooth, and one has to pay attention. Now she is talking about the growth of Christians themselves and the bearing of fruit in their own lives. Now she is talking about those in whose hearts Christians plant the gospel seed, and from whose lives, in turn, fruit must come.

"But always growth and fruit-bearing are God's to bring about. 'The plant grows by receiving that which God has provided to sustain its life. It sends down its roots into the earth. It drinks in the sunshine, the dew, and the rain. It receives the life-giving properties from the air. So the Christian is to grow by cooperating with the divine agencies' (*Christ's Object Lessons*, pp. 66, 67). This describes a calm dependence upon the Lord. The plant does not worry or fret about its growth. Nor should we.

"As we come down to the last six paragraphs of the chapter—the very section in which the crucial passage appears—the overriding emphasis turns to the need for us to look away from ourselves. The purpose for the reproduction of Christ's character in us, she says, is 'that it may be reproduced in others. The plant does not germinate, grow, or bring forth for itself.' Likewise, the Christian exists 'for the salvation of other souls. There can be no growth or fruitfulness in the life that is centered in self. If you have accepted Christ as a personal Saviour, you are to forget yourself, and try to help others' (*ibid.*, pp. 67, 68).

"In this call to total, unselfish ministry for others I find the key that unlocks the meaning of the passage before us. Clinching her point in a statement virtually parallel to the one we are studying here, she says: '*As you receive the Spirit of Christ — the Spirit of unselfish love and labor for others — you will grow and bring forth fruit. The graces of the Spirit will ripen in your character. Your faith will increase, your convictions deepen, your love be made perfect. More and more you will reflect the likeness of Christ in all that is pure, noble, and lovely*' (*ibid.*, p. 68; italics supplied).

"And what are these 'fruits,' these 'graces of the Spirit' that will ripen in our characters? None other than those Paul described in Galatians 5:22, 23, and which she cited: 'love, joy, peace, longsuffering, gentleness, goodness, faith, meekness, temperance.' As these 'fruits' come to full maturity, Christ, the heavenly husbandman, immediately puts in the sickle, she says, 'because the harvest is come' (*ibid.*, p. 69).

"Then follows, without a break, the principal statement we're studying here — repeating, in different words, the ripening, fruitbearing process just described. Clearly the thought is the same, and the two statements [highlighted on page 120 (bottom) and above] are part of a single whole.

"Accordingly, we may conclude that the reproduction of 'the character of Christ' in us is equivalent to our receiving 'the Spirit of Christ.' And 'the manifestation of [Christ] in His church' is equivalent to the development in us of 'the Spirit of unselfish love and labor for others.' We will then 'reflect the likeness of Christ in all that is pure, noble, and lovely.' When this occurs *in* us, and chain-reacts *through* us to multiplied millions around the world, the harvest will be ready, and Jesus will come to reap it.

"*So the emphasis in the* Christ's Object Lessons *statement is on incarnational ministry to others* — a ministry that is loving, compassionate, unselfish. No focus here on sinless perfection. 'The character of Christ' refers to 'the Spirit of unselfish love and labor for others.' Nor can we humanly manipulate the time of the harvest. 'Let man put forth his efforts to the utmost limit, he must still depend upon One who has connected the sowing and the reaping by wonderful links of His own omnipotent power' (*ibid.*, p. 63). The only way to 'hasten the coming of our Lord' is through incarnational ministry.

"Based on the intimate connection between the two extended highlighted statements in this section, we may now rephrase the first one as follows:

"*'Christ is waiting with longing desire for the manifestation of the Spirit of Christ in His church. When the Spirit of unselfish love and labor for others will have fully ripened in the character of His people, then He will come to claim them as His own.'*"

The editorial stayed close to the immediate context of Ellen White's remarks in *Christ's Object Lessons*. And so I did not provide any support from her other writings. But here are two statements that clearly validate the thrust of my interpretation here. Ponder them carefully, for they spell out what God requires of His people today. Don't think they're tangential, because they're not. They get to the very heart of the gospel and to what it means to be a Christian. They call for kindness, humility, unselfishness, love. These are tough. But that's where the rubber meets the road, as they say. 1. "*Unselfishness, the principle of God's kingdom, is the principle that Satan hates; its very existence he denies.* . . . To disprove Satan's claim is the work of Christ and all who bear His name.

"*It was to give in His own life an illustration of unselfishness that Jesus came in the form of humanity. And all who accept this principle are to be workers together with Him in demonstrating it in practical life*" (*Education*, p. 154; italics supplied).

2. "If we would *humble ourselves before God, and be kind and courteous and tenderhearted and pitiful,* there would be one hundred conversions to the truth where now there is only one. But, though professing to be converted, we carry around with us a bundle of self that we regard as altogether too precious to be given up. It is

our privilege to lay this burden at the feet of Christ *and in its place take the character and similitude of Christ*. The Saviour is waiting for us to do this" (*Testimonies*, vol. 9, pp. 189, 190; italics supplied).

The Bible Must Teach It

At this point, let me emphasize a methodological point of utmost importance. We need to understand clearly that whatever Ellen White says on perfection, sinless living, or any other topic, it is to be understood, according to her own insistence, against the background of Scripture. This means that every fundamental truth in her writings must be demonstrable on the basis of the Bible. "Our position and faith is in the Bible," she said. "And never do we want any soul to bring in the Testimonies ahead of the Bible" (*Evangelism*, p. 256; see also her other statements on pp. 256, 257).

In other words, if any point of our faith cannot be substantiated on the basis of Scripture alone, then it cannot be substantiated. And in *The Pharisee's Guide to Perfect Holiness*, Knight has shown that the requirement of absolute sinless perfection (à la Andreasen and others today) is not defensible — either from the Bible or from the writings of Ellen G. White (*Pharisee's Guide*, chapters 7-9).

Back to the Original Question

Now with all this background behind us, we're probably ready to return to the narrow question we're pursuing — whether God requires a different standard or quality of righteousness from the final generation of Christians that is above and beyond that required of previous generations.

Look again at the cardinal text used by those who espouse the idea of the absolute sinless perfection of a final remnant. And let's take it from the King James Version, the rendition they prefer: *"And in their mouth was found no guile: for they are without fault before the throne of God"* (Rev. 14:5).

The two key terms here, of course, are *guile* and *fault*.

No guile — Guile (Greek *pseudos* or as in some manuscripts *dolos*) refers to a lie, or a *falsehood*. The opposite of truth, the idea comes in for mention, as might be expected, throughout the Scriptures.

To give a brief sampling: The psalmist spoke disparagingly about those who "take delight in lies," blessing with their mouths, but cursing in their hearts (Ps. 62:4, NIV). "No one who practices deceit will dwell in my house," said the Lord through David. "No one who speaks falsely will stand in my presence" (Ps. 101:7, NIV). Isaiah, putting his finger on Israel's spiritual malady, mentioned "hands . . . stained with blood," "fingers [soiled] with guilt," and "*lips* [that] *have spoken lies*" (Isa. 59:3, NIV). And in a statement uncannily similar to the one in Revelation 14:5, the prophet Zephaniah declared: "The remnant of Israel will do no wrong; they will speak no lies, nor will deceit be found in their mouths" (Zeph. 3:13, NIV).

The significance of all these statements—and a veritable plethora of others we do not have room to cite—is that they were directed to contemporary Old Testament saints *in their time*, and so they represented God's expectations for His people way back then.

As just indicated, the Greek word *pseudos* (a *lie*, a *falsehood*) is the stark opposite of *aletheia* ("truth"), and characterizes the devil and all who follow him. This is the point Jesus tried to get across to the Jewish leaders who were seeking to assassinate Him: "You belong to your father, the devil. . . . He was a murderer from the beginning, *not holding to the truth*, for there is no truth in him. When he lies, he speaks his native language, *for he is a liar* and the *father of lies*" (John 8:44, NIV).

It is no wonder, then, that God's final remnant people are described as having no *pseudos*, no lie, in their mouths. They are people of truth, refusing to participate in the universal deception predicted for the last days, in which "evil men and impostors will proceed from bad to worse, deceiving and being deceived" (2 Tim. 3:13, NASB).

In contrast to such widespread fraudulence and deception, God's people will bear the characteristics of the One who declared: "I am the way, the *truth*, and the life" (John 14:6). "No lie was found in their mouths" (Rev. 14:5, NIV).

But if we understand what we're talking about, how can we argue that such a characteristic belongs only to the final generation of Christians? That would be nonsense. When Jesus saw

Nathanael, He said of him: "Behold an Israelite indeed, in whom is no guile [*∂olos*]!" (John 1:47). And it is interesting that this declaration was made at the beginning—not at the end—of Nathanael's walk with Jesus!

Philip, the one who brought Nathanael to Jesus, might not have recognized the qualities of his friend. Nor did Peter or the other disciples. But Jesus did. And He is the only one who can or needs to—the only one from whom it really counts. For "the Lord does not look at the things man looks at. Man looks at the outward appearance, but the Lord looks at the heart" (1 Sam. 16:7, NIV).

Without fault—So the 144,000 are people of truth, honesty, and integrity. "They are *without fault* before the throne of God" (Rev. 14:5).

The Greek word translated "without fault" here is *amomos*, meaning "unblemished." It conveys the idea "of the absence of defects in sacrificial animals," as in Numbers 6:14, for example (Arndt and Gingrich, *A Greek-English Lexicon of the New Testament and Other Early Christian Literature*, p. 47). In a moral and religious sense, the word means "blameless" (*ibid*., p. 48), the expression used in many modern translations—the New International Version, for example.

So the idea conveyed is that these saints on Mount Zion are without blemish, blame, or spot. God has accomplished His powerful work in them.

An Unchanging Requirement

Again, the issue for us at this point is not that of the saints' particular spiritual attainment, as such—whatever that is. Rather, it is whether that attainment characterizes only the final generation of Christians. And the answer, it seems to me, is that it does not.

Way back in hoary antiquity, God had described the patriarch Job as *"blameless [amemptos*, LXX] and *upright"* (Job 1:8; 2:3, NIV). And of Noah, who lived even earlier, the Bible says: "Noah was a righteous man, *blameless [teleios*, LXX] among the people of his time, and he walked with God" (Gen. 6:10, NIV).

There was really no need for such a description to be repeated again and again in the Bible. But we may correctly assume that the same could have been said of Abraham and Isaac and Isaiah and

Jeremiah and Daniel, of Shadrach, Meshach, and Abednego—and of a host of others in the Old Testament.

The general picture is the same when we come to the New Testament. Under a variety of terms, Paul (like John in Revelation 14:5) conveyed the idea of irreproachableness in regard to Christians in the first century who were waiting for the Lord's coming.

Thus he reminded the Corinthians that God "will keep you strong to the end, so that you will be *blameless* [*anegkletos*] on the day of our Lord Jesus Christ" (1 Cor. 1:8, NIV; cf. 1 Thess. 3:13). His prayer for the Philippians was that they should abound more and more "in knowledge and depth of insight . . . and may be *pure and blameless* [*aproskopos*] until the day of Christ" (Phil. 1:9, 10, NIV). This is why Christ died, he said—"to present you *holy* in his sight, *without blemish* [*amomos*] and free from accusation" (Col. 1:22, NIV).

There could be no question about the high divine expectation for first-century saints. God's goal for them was that they might become "*blameless* and *pure*, children of God *without fault* [*amemptos*] in a crooked and depraved generation, in which you shine like stars in the universe" (Phil. 2:15, NIV).

Elders and deacons were to be "blameless" [*anepileptos*; *anegkletos*] (1 Tim. 3:2; verse 10; 5:7; Titus 1:6, 7). But so also the entire church. Paul could not have been clearer on this point: "May God himself . . . sanctify you through and through. May your whole spirit, soul and body be kept *blameless* [*amemptos*] at the coming of our Lord Jesus Christ" (1 Thess. 5:23, NIV). And the recipients of Peter's letter were to "make every effort to be found *spotless, blameless* [*amometos*] and at peace" with God at His coming (2 Peter 3:14, NIV).

Incidentally, to suggest, as some might be tempted to do, that the admonitions of Paul and Peter in the last two references were based on their mistaken notion that the end was imminent would be disingenuous. What they demonstrate, rather, is that the message we need as we wait for the Advent is the same—whether we lived in the first century or live today. And the expectation is the same.

The Same High Standards
In view of the foregoing, we dare not interpret Revelation 14:5

in such a way as to make a spiritual distinction between the final remnant and the saints of previous centuries. What would distinguish the final saints will be the fact that like Job, they will maintain their loyalty and integrity through the most severe crucible of persecution in the history of the world. They will have gone through a most excruciating time of trouble, a time of trouble that will include the terrible seven last plagues (see Rev. 16). To maintain loyalty and integrity in the face of such an overwhelming crisis will indeed be a wonder to the universe.

But we have no warrant to believe that Revelation 14:5 describes a quality of righteousness essentially different from that required of previous generations. Notice these first-century admonitions.

"The night is nearly over; the day is almost here. So let us put aside the deeds of darkness and put on the armor of light. Let us behave decently, as in the daytime, not in orgies and drunkenness, not in sexual immorality and debauchery, not in dissension and jealousy. Rather, clothe yourselves with the Lord Jesus Christ, and do not think about how to gratify the desires of the sinful nature" (Rom. 13:12-14, NIV).

"Therefore, as God's chosen people, holy and dearly loved, clothe yourselves with compassion, kindness, humility, gentleness and patience. . . . And over all these virtues put on love, which binds them all together in perfect unity" (Col. 3:12-14, NIV).

"But the fruit of the Spirit is love, joy, peace, patience, kindness, goodness, faithfulness, gentleness and self-control. Against such things there is no law. Those who belong to Christ Jesus have crucified the sinful nature with its passions and desires. Since we live by the Spirit, let us keep in step with the Spirit" (Gal. 5:22-25, NIV).

"Christ loved the church and gave himself up for her to make her holy, cleansing her by the washing with water through the word, and to present her to himself as a radiant church, without stain or wrinkle or any other blemish, but holy and blameless" (Eph. 5:25-27, NIV).

"Finally, brothers, we instructed you how to live in order to please God, as in fact you are living. Now we ask you and urge you in the Lord Jesus to do this more and more. For you know what instructions we gave you by the authority of the Lord Jesus. It is God's will that you should be sanctified" (1 Thess. 4:1-7, NIV).

"It was he who gave some to be apostles, some to be prophets, some to be evangelists, and some to be pastors and teachers, to prepare God's people for works of service . . . until we all reach unity in the faith and in the knowledge of the Son of God and become mature, attaining to the whole measure of the fullness of Christ" (Eph. 4:11-13, NIV).

This last passage points to what careful Bible students, in light of all the facts, believe is the way to understand biblical perfection or holiness: as that of *maturity in Christ*.[3]

The Ultimate Test

When Jesus comes in glory with His mighty angels and the whole world gathers before Him, the issue, as Jesus Himself tells it, will be remarkably straightforward and down-to-earth. Like a shepherd separating his flock, He will divide all humanity into two groups—the "sheep" on the right, the "goats" on the left (Matt. 25:31-33).

"Then the King will say to those on his right, 'Come, you who are blessed by my Father; take your inheritance, the kingdom prepared for you since the creation of the world. For I was hungry and you gave me something to eat, I was thirsty and you gave me something to drink, I was a stranger and you invited me in, I needed clothes and you clothed me, I was sick and you looked after me, I was in prison and you came to visit me'" (verses 34-36, NIV). But the righteous do not say, "Whoopee! You noticed!" No. Because their goodness, far from being a show, had been spontaneous and unconscious, a genuine reflection of the love of Christ within. "Lord, when did we see you hungry and feed you?" they ask Him. "Or thirsty. . . . When did we see you a stranger . . . or needing clothes . . . ? When did we see you sick or in prison and go to visit you?" (verses 37, 38, NIV).

The King replies: "I tell you the truth, whatever you did for one of the least of these . . . , you did for me" (verse 40, NIV).

Said Ellen White: "Those whom Christ commends in the judgment may have known little of theology, but they have cherished

His principles. Through the influence of the divine Spirit they have been a blessing to those about them" (*The Desire of Ages*, p. 638).

And again: "Many feel that it would be a great privilege," she wrote, "to visit the scenes of Christ's life on earth. . . . But we need not go to Nazareth, to Capernaum, or to Bethany, in order to walk in the steps of Jesus. We shall find His footprints beside the sickbed, in the hovels of poverty, in the crowded alleys of the great city, and in every place where there are human hearts in need of consolation. In doing as Jesus did when on earth, we shall walk in His steps" (*ibid.*, p. 640).

So what does God require of us? The same as He required of His people in previous generations. It is quite possible, of course, that we'll be judged more severely than they, for we have been exposed to much greater light than they. But that is all.

Clearly, the controversy that has consumed the church over this issue is completely unwarranted. We have wasted valuable time. And we have discouraged many. If the hand of the devil is not in this, then he is not alive.

The irony is that the very One of whom angels sang "Glory to God . . . and on earth *peace*" has become, through the enemy's wicked cunning, the subject of a virtual civil war in some churches among us.

And my concern is that as worldliness and ignorance of the Bible and the writings of Ellen G. White become widespread among us, the specious reasoning of this perfectionist theology could well capture the allegiance of influential, well-meaning, and conscientious members and leaders among us, swinging the church into insidious heresy.

The time demands that we all open our Bibles and study for ourselves; that we spend whatever time is necessary to understand for ourselves the Spirit of Prophecy in its proper context; that we earnestly seek God for the Spirit, pleading that revival and reformation might begin with us, *personally*.

Our concerned brethren as well as our disaffected brethren do not thrive on nothing. The grist for their mill is the growing worldliness, the materialism, and—yes, let's say it—the liberalism in some sectors of the church. They are not completely off the beam when they charge that some of our pastors are "not preaching the message" anymore. You can visit a growing number of our churches for a long time without recognizing from the sermons that you were in a Seventh-day Adventist worship service.

This is a confusing time, a frustrating time, and, for many, a discouraging time. But we only compound the problem if we permit our frustration to lead us to embrace spurious and erroneous theology in the name of revival and reformation.

We must not lose our heads now. The present situation challenges each of us to keep awake, to keep alert, and, above all, to keep cool in the Lord!

"Jesus Christ is the same yesterday and today and forever" (Heb. 13:18, RSV). He is all-wise, all-powerful. The work is in His mighty hands. And His requirements are the same today as when He spoke them through the ancient prophet long ago: "He has showed you, O man, what is good. And what does the Lord require of you? To act justly and to love mercy and to walk humbly with your God" (Micah 6:8, NIV).

---

[1] (Andreasen, *Isaiah, the Gospel Prophet*, p. 82; *The Sabbath, Which Day?* pp. 246, 255; *The Book of Hebrews*, p. 468; cf. Adams, *The Sanctuary Doctrine*, p. 212.

[2] Incidentally, Wieland and Short refer here to *Testimonies to Ministers*, page 92, as the source of the phrase "obedience to all the commandments of God." From this the reader, not knowing the context, is led to believe that Ellen G. White's emphasis there was on an approach to righteousness that leads to obedience to all the commandments.

While she does refer to obedience as a manifestation of Christ's righteousness, the context makes clear that her purpose was to refocus the attention of the church on Christ Himself so that "the world should no longer say that Seventh-day Adventists talk the law, the law, but do not teach or believe Christ" (*Testimonies to Ministers*, p. 92).

This is just one example of the disrespect for context that pervades the writings of some who follow in Andreasen's theological footsteps. In this example, they have Ellen White give an emphasis that is exactly the opposite of what she intended.

[3] For an excellent study of the much misunderstand statement of Jesus "Be ye therefore perfect," see William Richardson, "The Unfavorite Text," *Adventist Review*, Oct. 14, 1993, pp. 8-10.

CAREFUL HOW YOU DRAW THE PARALLELS

God called Abraham from a relatively comfortable life in Mesopotamia to a special destiny in an unknown land. And untold numbers of commune leaders across the centuries have led their followers out into nowhere, with Abraham as their model.

God called Moses to lead out in the emancipation of a nation from the cruel grip of bondage. And through the years, untold numbers of liberation movements have drawn their inspiration from the Exodus, and the self-image of their leaders has been that of a new Moses.

Jesus denounced the hypocrisy of the Jewish leaders of His day. "Whited sepulchres" (Matt. 23:27), He called them—a "brood of vipers" (Matt. 12:34, NASB). And those who smite contemporary leaders with sharp-edged tongues today see themselves as standing in good company.

And there was Paul, champion of righteousness by faith. Confronting the stifling legalism of first-century Judaism, he trumpeted the freedom and power of the cross. And those today who somehow manage to include the word "cross" in every second sentence that they speak see themselves as twentieth-century Pauls, called out to rescue the church from legalism.

And there was James, who, in an effort to bring the righteousness of faith to the place where "the rubber meets the road," placed emphasis on the importance of works. Some today see themselves as modern-day Jameses, inveighing against the church for its alleged abandonment of the law.

Martin Luther rose up in the sixteenth century to confront an entrenched ecclesiastical establishment that had just about completely eclipsed the gospel. By his brave stance he changed—almost singlehandedly—the course of Christendom. And most reformers (or would-be reformers) since then have considered themselves modern-day Luthers, standing up to the powers that be.

Ellen G. White was only a shy teenager when God called her to her prophetic task. With only a third-grade education, she confounded all the odds, giving sober counsel to a growing movement, saving it again and again from danger and from irreparable theological blunders. Some today, however, making a virtue of her innocence and lack of formal training, have seen such qualities in themselves as badges of divine election and as proof positive that they too are special messengers to the remnant. To reject them is to follow in the footsteps of ancient Israel, which closed its ears and stiffened its neck against the Lord's prophets.

If I Could Send a Message . . .

If I could send one simple message to all these self-appointed "descendants" of the great and mighty prophets and reformers, it would be this: *Careful how you draw the parallels.* For although we may have in you a new Ellen White calling Laodicea to repentance, it is also possible that you may be one of those "foolish prophets" Ezekiel talked about, who "prophesy from their own inspiration" and who follow "their own spirit and have seen nothing" (Eze. 13:2, 3, NASB).

You may indeed be a new Martin Luther, standing up to the religious establishment. But then again, it is possible that you merely form a quartet with Korah, Dathan, and Abiram in opposition to some modern-day Moses (see Num. 16:1-35), that you are one of those spoken of in Jude 8—who "by dreaming" grandeur "reject authority" (NASB). Could it be that your vehemence and inordinate insistence on expounding righteousness by faith in every breath are simply a cover-up for something in your past? (Our hearts are tricky things, are they not?) Or perhaps you think of yourself as another James, calling the church back to its neglect of law and works. You may indeed be another James, but you may also be one of those Judaizers who dogged Paul's footsteps, maliciously accusing him of going soft on sin (see Rom. 3:8; 6:1). Sound familiar?

Perhaps you draw the ultimate parallel. You are a new messiah, raised up to denounce the modern scribes and Pharisees of Laodicea. Through video and audio, through printed word and spoken, your unrelenting censure falls upon "the brethren." But where are the tears—the tears that broke the voice of that first Messiah 2,000 years ago? (See *The Desire of Ages*, p. 353.)

Be Careful

Yes, there was Abraham, and there were Moses . . . and Jesus . . . and Paul . . . and Martin Luther . . . and Ellen White. But there were also Korah and Dathan and Abiram, and Balaam (Num. 22) and Hananiah (Jer. 28) and Jezebel (1 Kings 18:4, 19) and Hymenaeus (1 Tim. 1:18-20) and Philetus (2 Tim. 2:16, 17) and Phygelus and Hermogenes (2 Tim. 1:15) and Demas (2 Tim. 4:10) and Alexander the coppersmith (verse 13) and Judas and Jim Jones and David Koresh.

Naturally, we compare ourselves to the brightest and the best of yesteryear. But side by side with these shining ones were many turncoats and charlatans—even scoundrels. The selection is very precarious. So let's be careful how we draw the parallels.

This piece, slightly modified here, originally appeared in the *Adventist Review*, June 27, 1991, p. 4.

Index